# The Science
# Glass Ceiling

# The Science Glass Ceiling

*Academic Women Scientists
and the Struggle to Succeed*

**Sue V. Rosser**

Routledge
Taylor & Francis Group

NEW YORK AND LONDON

Published in 2004 by
Routledge
29 West 35th Street
New York, New York 10001
www.routledge-ny.com

Published in Great Britain by
Routledge
11 New Fetter Lane
London EC4P 4EE
www.routledge.co.uk

10 9 8 7 6 5 4 3 2 1

Rosser, Sue Vilhaur.
   The science glass ceiling : academic women scientists and the struggle to succeed / by Sue V. Rosser.
         p. cm.
Includes bibliographicasl references and index.
   ISBN 0-415-94512-7 (hardcover : acid-free paper) — ISBN 0-415-94513-5 (pbk. : acid-free paper)
   1. Women scientists—United States. 2. Discrimination in employment—United States. 3. Sex discrimination in employment—United States. I. Title.

Q130.R675 2004
331.4'815'0973—dc22                                    2003027571

*In memory of Barbara Lazarus*
*who gave much energy and professional expertise to women in science and*
*engineering*

# Contents

# Acknowledgments

During the last 6 years, 450 women scientists and engineers have been kind enough to respond to the e-mail questionnaire in which I sought their views on issues they face in their careers as well as their daily lives in the laboratory. I am grateful to each of these women for taking time from their very busy days and perpetual balancing of career and family to answer the questionnaire; I'm especially appreciative of the fifty respondents who permitted me to transgress further on their time by consenting to an in-depth telephone interview. I admire each of these women not only for what she has achieved in her own professional and personal life, but also for her clear commitment to making the path forward easier for other women scientists and engineers.

The support from the National Science Foundation, not only in the form of grant HRD -9807594, but also individuals involved with POWRE such as Joan Burelli, Mary Clutter, Sue Kemnitzer, Priscilla Nelson, and Bonnie Sheahan provided the impetus and momentum for this study. Jane Daniels, Director of the Clare Boothe Luce Program of the Henry Luce Foundation, not only provided access to the Clare Boothe Luce Professors, but she also co-authored part of chapter five with me. Without Jane, part of the study and book, would not have existed; I thoroughly enjoyed our collaboration.

Working with graduate students Mireille Zieseniss, Julie Montgomery, and Eliesh O'Neil Lane on statistical analyses of the data provided me with more excellent statistical expertise. Conversations with each of them gave me insights into life for the new generation of women scientists enmeshed in their graduate careers. If these three typify the next generation, the future looks bright indeed.

Routledge editor Ilene Kalish deserves a special note of thanks. In many ways I owe this book to her, since she was the one who convinced me to turn this project, that I had considered publishing only in journal articles, into a book. She suggested the interviews and prodded me to expand my writing and recommendations beyond my typical scientific, administrative style.

As always, a final note of gratitude goes to those closest to me on a daily basis. I am especially grateful to my assistant Judy Alexander, who helped me format the manuscript in general, and tables in particular. Without her handling of myriad administrative details, I would never have been able to complete the book. My family, Pat, Meagan, Caitlin, Ellen, Neil, Erica, Kraig, Kevin, Anoosh, and my mother provide the motivation and energy for this, as they do for all my work.

# Introduction

*I apologize for not writing sooner and responding to your questions. In fact, I'm not sure that I can respond to your first two questions in an objective way. I am experiencing a painful situation in my professional life and find I'm unable to write about it. Perhaps this situation is related to challenges facing women scientists in general or perhaps it is my individual experience. Nothing like this has happened to me before. I would be willing to speak with you over the phone and would appreciate the opportunity to do so. You can decide whether the information I provide is relevant and a reflection of the situation for women scientists in general or the institution where I'm located. Thank you.* — Sharon, research scientist from a prestigious Research I university on the West Coast

When I called her, Sharon began to explain the circumstances surrounding her current situation that led her to respond to the e-mail questionnaire sent to her with the quotation above. About two minutes into the conversation, she began to cry.

After receiving her Ph.D. and completing two postdocs in immunology, she had struggled with keeping her career as a bench scientist. After the birth of her two children, she had worked part time and then full time in a group with about eight other individuals. The head of the group told her that it was time for her to become independent. Based on his suggestion, she wrote and obtained the National Science Foundation (NSF) grant. Although the project funded was related to the work she had done in the group, suddenly she found herself marginalized from the group members, who no longer wanted to discuss results with her, and moved to a different location, with all major equipment, including her printer, removed. Although her grant paid her salary and some expenses, she needed the group for equipment and more importantly for collegial interaction and support. She has been made to feel unwanted with no control over her space and equipment. Although individuals in other institutions seem interested in her work, she cannot move because of family constraints. She is wondering whether she can still pursue her career as a scientist, despite the fact that she has a grant to support the work. As the quotation above suggests, she also wonders whether this is something only she faces at her individual institution or whether these circumstances commonly plague women scientists throughout academia.

> In response to that question, I was so relieved to hear that other senior women scientists are frustrated and thinking of dropping out of science or switching to something else. I had thought it was only me and that probably it was my fault that I just couldn't take it any more. Although your talk focused on attracting undergraduate women to science, afterwards several of the women faculty who had been here for a long time kept talking about the issues raised by the question from the audience about the satisfaction of more senior women scientists with their careers. All but one of us admitted that we were seriously thinking of getting out in one way or another. In a way it made me feel better to know that I wasn't the only one thinking these things. On the other hand, it was pretty depressing to realize that all of us smart, successful women scientists were seriously thinking of making a change.

> Being at a small liberal arts college, we're not as isolated as some of my colleagues from graduate school who went to research institutions. I did manage to have a family, and I still enjoy teaching, although prepping my own labs, the large number of contact hours semester after semester, and all the committee work I get because I'm a woman, have left me pretty burnt out. Still, I notice that most of my male colleagues have managed to keep their research going, at least at some low level, but mine went by the way several years ago when my kids were little. I regret it though and wonder sometimes if there is any way I could get it back. I wish there were some way that either the college could help me or maybe there is some program sponsored

by a foundation that might make this possible for me and the other women. If not, I'm not sure how long the others and I can hang in here. — Jane, a tenured full professor at a small, northeastern prestigious liberal arts college

These women ask: Is it my individual failing as a woman and a scientist that makes me question the possibility that I can have a successful, happy career in academia? Are the problems I'm having the result of barriers that most women scientists at my institution (and most institutions) face as we try to build reasonable personal and professional lives?

As a dean at a Research I institution for five years now and as a scholar who has worked for a quarter of a century on theoretical and applied problems of attracting and retaining women in science and engineering, I have heard the expression of these doubts and dilemmas in a variety of forms from diverse women scientists and engineers in all types of institutions. Virtually all of the women are united in their love for science and desire to sustain their interest in the physical, natural world that attracted them to the study of science initially. Most would like nothing better than to pursue that love through their research and teaching in academia. But as the women themselves know, and as the statistics about gender and science document, more women than men are lost from science at every level of the pipeline. The women scientists question whether their individual choices, decisions, and will power, or institutional obstacles and barriers, prevent them from fulfilling their research potential and career goals.

In fact, for many years, most of the research approaches, as well as the approach of the national funding agencies, suggested that the women and science issues/problems resulted from individual choices and decisions. Research on gender differences in the amount of time taken to achieve tenure, publication productivity, and receipt of prestigious awards, coupled with assertiveness training and reentry programs for women, led to the "woman as deficient" model. Not surprisingly, many women internalized this model and questioned whether something was wrong with them as individuals because of the obstacles to success in their academic scientific careers. At best, they lost confidence in themselves and wondered where they personally had gone wrong, as did the women quoted above. At worst, they dropped out of academia and science.

But circumstances are changing. More recently, academic institutional leaders, funding agencies, and the scientific professional societies have begun to recognize that a focus on institutional change might be needed to lower the barriers and remove obstacles to increase the number of women scientists. After all, failure to change the percentage of women significantly by applying individual solutions suggests the need for systemic institutional changes to facilitate the careers of individual women scientists and engineers.

In March 1999 the Massachusetts Institute of Technology released "A Study on the Status of Women Faculty in Science at MIT," creating a stir that spread far beyond the institutional boundaries of MIT. Five years earlier senior biology professor Nancy Hopkins, (1999) initiated the collection of evidence documenting that the 15 tenured women faculty in science had received lower salaries and fewer resources for research than their male colleagues. Dean Robert Birgeneau recognized that in addition to salary disparities, the data in the report revealed systemic, subtle biases in space, start-up packages, access to graduate students, and other resources that inhibited the careers of women scientists relative to their male counterparts. Release of the report struck a nerve with administrators and women faculty on campuses across the nation. Headlines such as "Women at MIT Create a Movement for Female Academics" that appeared in *The Chronicle of Higher Education* (December 3, 1999), also echoed in *Science*, the *New York Times*, and countless other publications, fueled questions about the status of women scientists at other academic institutions and in the broader profession.

More than 1 year later, MIT president Charles Vest hosted a meeting of the presidents, chancellors, provosts, and 25 women scientists from the most prestigious research universities (California Institute of Technology, MIT, University of Michigan, Princeton, Stanford, Yale, University of California at Berkeley, Harvard, and University of Pennsylvania) at MIT. At the close of the meeting on January 29, 2001, they issued the following statement: "Institutions of higher education have an obligation, both for themselves and for the nation, to fully develop and utilize all the creative talent available," the leaders said in a unanimous statement. "We recognize that barriers still exist" for women facult. They agreed:

> *To analyze the salaries and proportion of other university resources provided to women faculty,*
> *To work toward a faculty that reflects the diversity of the student body,*
> *To reconvene in about a year "to share the specific initiatives we have undertaken to achieve these objectives,"*
> *To "recognize that this challenge will require significant review of, and potentially significant change in, the procedures within each university, and within the scientific and engineering establishments as a whole."*
> *(Campbell, 2001, p. 1)*

For the first time, in public and in print, the leaders of the nation's most prestigious universities suggested that institutional barriers have prevented women scientists and engineers from having a level playing field and that science and engineering might need to change to accommodate women.

Almost simultaneously, the NSF initiated ADVANCE, a new awards program, which provided funding of $17 million for 2001. The program offers an award for institutional, rather than individual, solutions to empower women to participate fully in science and technology. The NSF encouraged institutional, rather than individual, solutions because of "increasing recognition that the lack of women's full participation at the senior level of academe is often a systemic consequence of academic culture" (NSF, 2001b, p. 2). Under ADVANCE, Institutional Transformation Awards, ranging up to $750,000 per year for up to 5 years, were granted to promote the increased participation and advancement of women; and Leadership Awards recognized the work of outstanding organizations of individuals and enabled them to sustain, intensify, and initiate new activity (NSF, 2001b).

These public admissions by the most prestigious and mainstream universities and foundations in American that they must become more women-centered and that parts of their own institutions have remained closed to most women serve as a major step forward. Making this shift from a male-centered profession will require significant institutional changes to empower women scientists and engineers. The changes will not happen overnight. It is an especially daunting task because of the historical, statistical, and cultural traditions that have built the university to fit male needs, developmental stages, and interests. As women have entered the university, we have fought to change these male-centered traditions to make them more female friendly, but the level playing field still does not exist as the following section attests.

### Profile of Women in Science and Engineering

Although attempts to produce a more female-friendly environment have encountered substantial resistance, the most significant changes have occurred in parts of the university where the most women have been for the longest time. Historically, women were not permitted to enroll in institutions of higher education; the first coeducational colleges and universities emerged in the United States in 1833 with many of the Midwest land grant universities established as coeducational from their inception in the 1860s (Solomon, 1985). The women's colleges in the East and South provided important opportunities for women students to receive an excellent education; they provided virtually the only opportunities for women faculty to teach and pursue scholarly research (Glazer & Slater, 1987). As late as 1966, women constituted 43% of undergraduates, 34% of MS, and 12% of Ph.D. students (NSF, 2000, table 3-12) in all U.S. institutions.

Currently, 56% of undergraduates (NSF, 2000, table 1-5) and 54% of graduate students (NSF, 2000, table 3-12) are women. In these days of attention to statistics and interest in meeting the needs of the student as consumer, universities have accommodated some practices for the statistical majority, who are women students. However, resistance to both curricular and extracurricular changes for equity can be seen, in part, in the struggle of women's studies to become departments (Carroll, 2001; DeGroot & Maynard, 1993; Pryse et al., 1999; Zimmerman, 2000) and women's sports (Heckman, 1997; Sandler, 1997) to obtain equity and legitimacy.

In some disciplines and even in whole colleges within a given university, women students remain in the minority. Although the numbers of women majoring in scientific and technological fields has increased since the 1960s to reach almost 50% in 1998 (NSF, in press, table 3.4),

**TABLE 1** Women as a Percentage of Degree Recipients in 1996 by Major Discipline and Group

| | ALL FIELDS | ALL SCIENCE & ENGINEERING | PSYCHOLOGY | SOCIAL SCIENCES | BIOLOGY | PHYSICAL SCIENCES | GEOSCIENCES | ENGINEERING |
|---|---|---|---|---|---|---|---|---|
| Percentage of Bachelor's degrees received by women | 55.2 | 47.1 | 73.0 | 50.8 | 50.2 | 37.0 | 33.3 | 17.9 |
| Percentage of MS degrees received by women | 55.9 | 39.3 | 71.9 | 50.2 | 49.0 | 33.2 | 29.3 | 17.1 |
| Percentage of Ph.D. degrees received by women | 40.0 | 31.8 | 66.7 | 36.5 | 39.9 | 21.9 | 21.7 | 12.3 |

*Source:* NSF 2000 Appendix table 2–6, p. 119, Appendix table 4–3, p. 170, Appendix table 4–11, p. 188.
*Note:* For bachelor's degrees, the data used in the introductory chapter are for 1998 and those for the Ph.D. are for 1997. In this table, 1996 was used because those were the only data available for all 3 degree levels.

the percentage of women in computer science, the physical sciences, and engineering remains small. Table 1 documents the tremendous range within the science and engineering disciplines for 1996. In 1998 women received 74% of the bachelor's degrees in psychology but only 19% of the degrees in engineering (NSF, in press, table 3.4). The percentage of computer science degrees awarded to women actually dropped from 37% in 1984 to 20% in 1999 (Eisenberg, 2001).

The percentage of graduate degrees in these fields earned by women remained lower. While women earned 56% of the MS degrees in all fields, they earned only 39% of the degrees in science and engineering fields, even when the social sciences are included. Table 1 reveals a similar range for MS degree recipients, with women receiving 72% of the MS degrees in psychology but only 17% in engineering. Although women earned 40% of the Ph.D. degrees in all fields, they earned 33% of the Ph.D. degrees in sciences and engineering. Table 1 shows the range from a low of 12% in engineering to a high of 67% in psychology.

Women faculty still do not represent a statistical majority of professors overall; data reported in 2000, based on 1995 figures by the Commission on Professionals in Science and Technology, show that women constituted 35% of faculty overall, with the vast majority holding positions at the lowest ranks in the less prestigious institutions. Table 2 documents the percentage of women faculty holding various ranks within each disciplinary grouping and reveals an inverse relationship between rank and percentage of women. At all institutions, only 18% of women hold the highest rank of full professor. The data in table 3 indicate significantly fewer women than men also hold tenure at both four year and research institutions. At four year institutions, 71% of men and 47% of women held tenure, while at universities, 75% of men and 47% of women faculty had tenure (CPST, 2000, Table 5-10). With their male colleagues continuing to remain as the majority and in the more powerful positions, women faculty have met considerable resistance to requests for policies to stop the tenure-clock during childbearing, on-site daycare, and dual-career hiring to make the university more female-friendly. Increasingly tight economic times and fiscal constraints make it less likely that institutional administrations will respond positively to such family-friendly policy requests.

**TABLE 2** Percentage of Women Doctoral Scientists and Engineers in Academic Institutions by Field and Rank in 1997

| | ALL FIELDS | PSYCHOLOGY | SOCIAL SCIENCES | BIOLOGY/ LIFE SCIENCES | PHYSICAL SCIENCES | ENGINEERING | MATH & COMPUTER SCIENCES |
|---|---|---|---|---|---|---|---|
| Assistant Professor | 36.9 | 61.0 | 39.6 | 36.7 | 26.1 | 13.7 | 24.1 |
| Associate Professor | 25.7 | 44.3 | 32.4 | 22.9 | 13.5 | 6.3 | 14.3 |
| Full Professor | 11.6 | 22.5 | 14.9 | 13.1 | 4.2 | 1.4 | 6.7 |
| Total (includes Instructor/ Lecturer) | 25.1 | 43.1 | 28.3 | 27.8 | 13.3 | 6.5 | 14.2 |

*Source:* Commission on Professionals in Science and Technology (CPST), 2000, table 5–1.

**TABLE 3** Percentage of Men and Women with Tenure in Academic 1996–97

| | MEN | WOMEN |
|---|---|---|
| All institutions | 71.8 | 51.6 |
| Four-year institutions | 70.9 | 46.9 |
| Universities | 74.6 | 47.4 |

*Source:* Commission on Professionals in Science and Technology (CPST), 2000, table 5–10.

The small number of women receiving degrees in the sciences and engineering results in an even smaller percentage of women faculty in these fields: For example, only 20% of science and engineering faculty at four year colleges and universities are women; 10% of the full professors, 22% of the associate professors, and 33% of the assistant professors in science and engineering at these institutions are women (NSF, 2000, Table 5-15). Although many have read these statistics as suggesting that women will reach parity with men in these fields as they advance through the ranks, other information indicates that more substantial changes must occur to make the climate more female friendly to retain senior women in these fields.

Perhaps it is not surprising that the male dominance in these fields is reflected not only in their statistical majority, but also in a continued tradition of male-centered approaches in labs, practices, and cultures. The extent to which these approaches, practices, and cultures present institutional barriers for women scientists and engineers has recently been underlined through the MIT report released in 1999 and recent anecdotal reports that some women scientists actively choose to avoid research universities because of the hostile climate (Schneider, 2000). Recent data document that women make up 40% of tenure-track science faculty in undergraduate institutions (Curry, 2001). Although the bulk of science and technology research occurs at institutions formerly classified as Research I, less lab space, lower salaries, and fewer prestigious opportunities exemplify the kinds of barriers typical for women as compared to men. A dawning recognition that these barriers can best be addressed by institutional, rather than individual, changes became evident from the statement released after the MIT meeting on January 29, 2001, and from the focus of the ADVANCE initiative from NSF.

### Focus of this Study

This book presents quantitative and qualitative data that elucidate the problems and opportunities surrounding the careers and daily lives of 450 women scientists and engineers at academic institutions. All of these women had received external validation of their potential for successful careers both through their employment at liberal arts colleges and research institutions and by receiving at least one of two prestigious awards: either a National Science Foundation (NSF) Professional Opportunities for Women in Research and Education (POWRE) award or a Clare Boothe Luce Professorship award. More than 70% of the women found "balancing work with family" to be the most significant challenge facing women scientists and engineers.

The balancing act between career and family varies for individual women, depending upon when or whether they decide to have children and their obligations to elderly parents or inlaws. If they delay childbearing, some become part of the "sandwich" generation, tending both to children and aging parents simultaneously.

> At the risk of stereotyping, I think that women generally struggle more with the daily pull of raising a family or caring for elderly parents, and this obviously puts additional demands on their time. This is true for younger women, who may struggle over the timing of having and raising children, particularly in light of a ticking tenure clock, but also for more senior women, who may be called upon to help aging parents (their own or inlaws). Invariably they manage, but not without guilt. (2000 respondent 63)

Since more than 60% of women scientists are married to men scientists, finding positions for two people poses another challenge. This becomes particularly difficult in fields such as physics where about 68% of women physicists are married to male scientists; whereas 17% of male physicists are married to female scientists (MacNeil & Sher, 1999). Because many of these couples meet in graduate school, they seek positions in the same research area or subdiscipline.

> In contrast to other issues related to women choosing careers in science, the two-body problem has received far too little public as well as governmental attention. Universities are basically tackling the problem individually; some act progressively, others don't. The fates of these capable women depend too much on the individual deans or department chairs involved. (1998 respondent 45)

Further details about the problems, challenges, and hopes for possible solutions emerged from in-depth interviews with a sample of about 40 of these women. I analyzed their responses into seven broad fields within science in order to show that in addition to balancing career and family, there are similar problems across the disciplines, such as time management issues, isolation and lack of camaraderie, mentoring due to small numbers, gaining credibility and respectability from peers, and two career placements. There were some differences among disciplines uncovered. Because of the low numbers of women, isolation and lack of camaraderie/mentoring are particularly acute problems for women in fields such as engineering, physics, and computer science.

> In my field [concrete technology], women are so poorly represented that being female certainly creates more notice for you and your work, particularly when presenting at conferences. This can be beneficial, as recognition of your research by your peers is important for gaining tenure; it can also add to the already large amount of pressure on new faculty. (2000 respondent 70)

> I've noticed some problems in particular institutions I have visited (or worked at) where women were scarce. As a single woman, I have sometimes been viewed as "available," rather than as a professional coworker. That can be really, really irritating. I assume that single men working in a location where male workers are scarce can face similar problems. In physics and astronomy, usually the women are more scarce. (1997 respondent 26)

> There are almost no women in my field, no senior women, and open harassment and discrimination are very well accepted and have never been discouraged in any instance I am aware of. (1998 respondent 53)

> The discrimination we continue to face in the workplace. We seem to be making virtually no gains in terms of rates at which women are granted tenure or promotion to full professor. The older I get, the more depressing these statistics become. Women's research is often marginalized. Women's approaches are not recognized. Men scientists want to judge women by "their" standard (i.e. the white male way of doing things!). Most men have no appreciation for the power and privilege of their whiteness and maleness. (1999 respondent 70)

Perhaps the most exciting evidence to emerge from the data was the potential for the new ideas and approaches women might contribute to science and engineering because of their experience as women.

The most significant challenge I face is favoring "hacker" experience. In the computer science discipline in which I work, respect is conferred upon those who possess knowledge obtained primarily through countless hours investigating the nuances of hardware and operating systems. To many in my peer group, this is a relaxing hobby and way of life. Though I learn these nuances as I need them for my research, outside of my work I read literature, am deeply interested in social issues and am committed to being involved in my child's life. I see this alternate experience base as an asset to my field. As Rob Pike of C language fame recently said, "Narrowness of experience leads to narrowness of imagination." But for now, the perception is still tilted against me. (1999 respondent 68)

I've built a project and a lab with a group of female scientists. It was a mere coincidence (or was it?) to form an interdisciplinary research visualization group in applied medicine (e.g. virtual surgical training, teaching anatomy via 3D visualization, at [my university's] medical school). Because our group consists of computer scientists, computational linguists, cognitive psychologists, anatomists, we had to establish communication between these disciplines ... somehow we managed to develop an amazing climate to collaborate and also attract female graduate students to do research with us. (1998 respondent 50)

Some women can manage to construct a small, empowering environment within a larger hostile environment.

I find the laboratory climate more liberal than, say, the "office climate." I also feel autonomous, powerful and free in this environment (maybe it's because I get to use power tools?). In the laboratory climate, I am able to create and build. I am also able to ask for help and delegate responsibility. Sometimes my colleagues ask me for help. There is a hierarchical structure at the laboratory in which I work, but it is more fluid, roles switch as projects come through. Sometimes I will take the lead and other times I will follow. In terms of my

> career, working in a laboratory offers a fantastic opportunity to work
> alone, work with a large group and manage a project, offer support to
> a colleague, and to build a small community. (1997 respondent 27)

The examples of different approaches to problems, smoothly functioning interdisciplinary collaborations, and positive laboratory environments underline the benefits of having women working in the fields of science and technology. Cutting-edge research in science and engineering today needs innovative approaches to complex problems that are more likely to be solved by interdisciplinary teams that require a supportive environment to thrive.

### Changing Science

This transitional moment, when focus shifts from solutions for the individual to institutional change, compels me to write this book. As the quotations at the beginning of this chapter reveal, when individual women scientists feel mistreated, isolated, and undervalued, they tend to blame themselves or at least question whether they or the institution should be faulted. I write this book for the women scientists because I have substantial data demonstrating that women in all fields of science and engineering in a diverse set of institutions encounter similar barriers and problems. The problem is not with the women, but with the institution of science as currently practiced. I hope this book will make that clear and will offer a way forward.

I also write this book for the leaders of those institutions who seek to lower the barriers to attract and retain more women in science. University presidents, heads of foundations and funding agencies, and chairs of National Academy committees and professional societies demonstrate eagerness to understand what the obstacles are so they can attempt to remove them. What I have found reveals some of the parameters of the problems and the barriers, and ultimately provides a step toward their solution. There are policy recommendations here for the leaders of institutions, funding agencies, and professional societies seeking to mitigate the difficulties and challenges currently experienced by women scientist and engineers.

To maintain its leadership in science and engineering in the face of increasing global competition, the United States cannot afford to lose these highly creative and well-trained women scientists and engineers. The changes in student and immigration visas brought on in the wake of September 11 have reduced the availability of reliable international scientists that the United States has typically used to fill its technical and scientific workforce in the past decade. Defining and removing barriers becomes critical to allow women scientists who are passionate about their work not only to survive but to thrive in academic institutions.

# CHAPTER 1
## WHO ARE THE WOMEN SCIENTISTS?

Women scientists and engineers, like women in other professions and their male counterparts in science and engineering, desire to have a satisfying career that enables them to explore the secrets of the physical, natural world while also leading a rewarding family life, rearing children, having a stable relationship with a partner, fulfilling obligations to their community, or pursuing interests important to them. Everyone struggles to turn this desire into a reality in daily life.

Many women wonder when, if ever, to have children. Having them early, while still in school, may make starting a career more difficult. Waiting until after achieving tenure increases the potential for "a high-risk pregnancy." Some women decide early on that they must work at a Research I university to have access to the equipment they require for their research; others pursue the Ph.D. because they love teaching undergraduates and can't wait to return to the environment of a small liberal arts college. For most, the type of institution that will best facilitate their careers and families becomes one of the pieces of the puzzle. Many attempt to pursue their personal career goals in tandem with those of a partner or spouse. Some have immigrated to the United States and attempt to intertwine this new culture and environment with that of the country of their birth. No clear-cut path or magic key opens success and satisfaction for all women. People puzzle over the timing of career and family decisions. As the subtitle of the anthology *Journeys of Women in Science and Engineering* (1997) by Susan Ambrose, Kristin Dunkle, Barbara Lazarus, Indira Nair, and Deborah Harkus suggests, there are *No Universal Constants*.

To learn more about the intertwining of the professional and personal career paths, I interviewed a sample of the almost 400 women who had received NSF POWRE awards and responded to an e-mail questionnaire that I sent; I neither had access to nor requested information regarding race/ethnicity, nationality, age, rank, marital or parental status, although sometimes the respondent revealed these in the e-mail response or interview. Individuals in the selected sample received the following e-mail:

E-mail Request to Interview

In 1998–99 [this varied, depending upon the year of the award] you were kind enough to respond to a brief e-mail questionnaire as an NSF POWRE awardee. As part of an ongoing effort to understand significant issues in the careers of women scientists and engineers, you are being asked to volunteer to participate in a research project as a follow-on to the e-mail questionnaire to which you responded. You have been selected as one of 40 volunteers to be interviewed from the almost 400 respondents to the initial questions.

The project consists of one telephone interview lasting approximately 45 minutes with me, arranged via e-mail at a time that is mutually convenient for both you and me. During the interview you will be asked 5 questions exploring significant issues women scientists and engineers face in their careers and/or laboratories, as well as the impact that you perceive that receiving the award has had on your career. Up to 7 follow-on questions may be asked to clarify your responses to the 5 general questions.

Although this study has no known risks, you may refuse to respond to any question that you prefer not to answer for any reason. If you are harmed as a result of being in this study, please contact me. Neither the Principal Investigator (me) nor Georgia Institute of Technology have made provision for payment of costs associated with any injury resulting from participation in this study. All information concerning you obtained from the interview, as well as your responses to the previous questionnaire, will be kept private. If information and quotations from your interview and/or questionnaire are published, you will be identified by number only and the information will be written in a way that maintains your confidentiality and prevents recognition of you individually. You will not be paid nor are there any costs to you by participating.

Your voluntary participation in this project is extremely important to shed light on issues important to the careers of women scientists and engineers. You may not benefit directly by participating in this study, but by underlining solutions, practices, and policies to attract and retain women in science and engineering, the results of this research should benefit institutions, funding agencies, and professional societies seeking to remove institutional barriers, policies, and practices that serve as obstacles for women scientists and engineers.

Please reply to this e-mail, indicating your willingness to participate in the interview. You may indicate times that would be especially convenient for the interview or I will request that information in a subsequent e-mail.

I would be happy to answer any questions you have about this project. Please contact me by e-mail or phone me at (xxx)xxx-xxxx for answers to any questions. If you have questions about your rights as a research subject please contact Alice Basler at (xxx)xxx-xxxx.

Thank you for your participation.
Sue V. Rosser, Dean and Professor
Ivan Allen College
Georgia Institute of Technology
Atlanta, GA 30332

Most responded to the e-mail immediately, and we negotiated a mutually convenient time for me to phone them. Recognizing that each woman was likely to have a fascinating, but unique story and set of experiences, in order to provide some uniformity for comparison among individuals, I asked each interviewee the same five questions:

Telephone Interview Questions

1. Tell me the story of your professional career, including the major influences, opportunities, and challenges that enabled you to become the woman scientist (engineer) you are today.

Example follow-on/clarification: Since you suggest that you are an exception, what do you think are the most significant issues/challenges/opportunities facing women scientists today as they plan their careers?

2. How did receiving an NSF POWRE award impact your career?

Example follow-on clarification: Although it seems that the award was very positive for your career overall, did it have any negative impacts?

3. Do you think that the POWRE award you received helped to attract and retain other women in science?

Example follow-on clarification: What other sorts of programs at your institution or others have you found to also be useful in attracting and retaining women in science (engineering)?

4. What are the key institutional barriers to women in science and engineering having successful academic careers?

Example follow-on clarification: What solutions can institutions pursue to remove those barriers? Does your institution have an NSF ADVANCE award? If so, are you involved with ADVANCE?

5. What is the overall climate for women in your specific discipline?

Example follow-on clarification: How does the laboratory climate (or its equivalent in your subdiscipline) impact upon the careers of women scientists?

The 11 interviews chosen for this chapter from the 40 women scientists and engineers interviewed for the project reveal multiple paths to success. This chapter only includes the interviews of NSF POWRE awardees; Chapter 5 includes interviews with Clare Boothe Luce professors. Although women scientists and engineers work at a variety of types of institutions, ranging from women's colleges through comprehensive public institutions to elite private Research I universities, the POWRE awardees tend to work at larger institutions. The majority came from public universities. Some always knew that they would become a scientist or engineer; others combined their interest in humanities, social sciences, or arts with science and engineering. They entered graduate school immediately after college or after a successful career in another field. Some had their children late, after becoming a tenured full professor, while others became mothers in graduate school. The element common to all is their love for their work in science and engineering and their commitment to and love for their families. The names of the individuals have been changed throughout the book to protect their privacy.

### Choosing Educational and Work Environments for Family-Friendliness: Physicist Jane Fields

As the data in Tables 1, 2, and 3 reveal, physics remains one of those fields with very few women, especially in the professoriate. Deciding to begin a family while still in graduate school, Jane Fields consciously sought mentors and laboratory environments that she thought would be supportive of her decision to combine family and work. As the following interview with Jane suggests, even though her department does not require continuous, major funding to achieve tenure, time demands still pose a challenge for balancing career and family.

> Jane Fields liked science and math during high school so when she entered college she was fairly certain that she wanted to go into science. During her freshman year at a very prestigious private Research I institution in the Northeast, she took chemistry, but the physics class she took as a sophomore really captured her interest.
>
> After undergraduate school she took a year off and taught high school chemistry before entering graduate school in physics at a prestigious Research I public institution in California. She was fortunate to have a good advisor who was supportive of her even when she had kids while in graduate school. In selecting him, she had applied the office test—students sleeping in the office/lab signaled a negative omen. Although Jane categorizes herself in the group of women for whom seeing other women as role models doesn't matter, she did remark that a nice group of women graduate students got together a couple of times each semester and that one or two women faculty often joined them.

Being 4 months pregnant with her second child as she searched for a postdoc became another test that she applied to determine the suitability of a lab. She ended up at a prestigious technical institution in the Northeast where she had a supportive male advisor during the 2 years of her postdoc.

As she applied for academic positions, she noted departments that did not require having continuous funding. Although the Ivy league institution where she is a faculty member does not have that requirement, she finds that the five-course per year teaching load, large number of committees on which she serves, and absence of graduate students make it very difficult to conduct the excellent research demanded to achieve tenure in less than a 50-hour workweek. She hopes she will be successful in her tenure bid later this year.

The NSF POWRE award permitted Jane to buy what she needed for her lab that had not been included in the start-up package provided by her institution. She believes that for many women, seeing women in science encourages them to enter the profession. For example, she taught in all three introductory courses of the first physics class to graduate more than 50% women. She reaches out to elementary schools and has an NSF grant to run a summer science camp for 14- to 16-year-old girls.

Jane perceives time as the biggest barrier for women in science who wish to have families. Unless work is limited to 50 hours per week and the tenure system is changed, she doubts that a significant number of women will enter science. Her typical day consists of 10 hours of work devoted to teaching, research, and service, 6 hours for her family, and 8 hours for sleeping, eating, and bathing. In short, she lacks adequate time.

Jane believes that women in physics receive equal treatment, although their minority status makes them very visible. However, women do experience systemic discrimination because of the expectations for length of the workday and -week for physics, which is unrealistic when coupled with family responsibilities.

### Going Abroad as an Undergraduate Confirms Scientific Field Interest: Botanist Suzanne Hausmann

In contrast to Jane Fields, Suzanne Hausmann delayed having a child until she obtained a faculty position. Despite that delay and the higher percentage of women in botany compared to physics, Suzanne still felt isolated since few faculty in her department had children. In her interview, Suzanne emphasizes the crucial role that experiences in Europe had on attracting her initially to the field of botany and in midcareer, stimulating her to flourish.

Suzanne Hausmann attributes her interest in the natural world, developed from hiking, camping, and spending time outdoors as a child, as the initial motivator for her to become a scientist. While an undergraduate at a large, Midwestern Research I institution, she became fascinated by photosynthesis, finding chloroplasts really interesting.

Despite her fascination, she wonders in retrospect whether her interest in botany would have held had she not gone to Germany during her junior year of college. In contrast to the United States, where botany appears to be on the decline, veneration for the study of botany remained in Germany and Europe in the early 1970s. In Germany, Suzanne first used electron microscopy.

After graduation, she moved to the big city and worked as a technician. Since she did not come from an academic family, the idea of graduate school didn't occur to her, until she received encouragement from the folks in the lab where she worked. While attending graduate school at the world-renowned private institution across town, she thought little about gender. With other women as half of her fellow students, she felt no bias as a graduate student. Time spent at Woods Hole in the summer provided her with very strong female role models who influenced her and motivated her to stay in graduate school.

During her postdoctoral experience at a large Southern university, she encountered her first experience of gender bias. At that institution, it seemed that men were in the labs, and women were in the offices as secretaries. In fact, people had difficulty distinguishing her from the only other female postdoc, since both of them wore jeans.

When she obtained her faculty position, she found that she was the second woman in the department in this large Research I public institution in the West. She became the first woman there, some 10 years ago, to have a child. At the time Suzanne gave birth to her child, it was a lonely and somewhat isolating experience, although now the department seems to be experiencing an explosion of children born to the faculty.

The receipt of the NSF POWRE award not only permitted her to turn her research in a different direction, it also allowed Suzanne to return to Europe. There she solidified multiple international collaborations and attended small European meetings, where she gave some 17 presentations and expanded her network. Since she was in Europe, she could not verify that her receipt of the POWRE award influenced other women to go into science; however, whenever she gives a talk, another woman from the audience will always come up to speak with her, often saying that it's important to see a successful woman scientist who runs her own lab and does science.

Although she finds the climate for women in her discipline to be good, and that at her institution to be improving, she still finds some bias against women as power holders. Some concrete problems such as the lower salaries of women compared to men and the issues surrounding parenting and dual-career couples may be addressed by changing institutional policies. Suzanne believes that a major difficulty for women is that they are not in the loop of informal conversations. This causes them to miss out on crucial tidbits of information such as the possibility of approaching the dean for cost-sharing, negotiating counteroffers, and obtaining equipment through the use of year-end money. Mentoring from senior colleagues helps junior women learn the ropes.

### Having the Tenacity to Persist: Chemical Engineer Colleen O'Neal

Like Suzanne, Colleen O'Neal also experienced isolation, but not as a result from the struggle to balance career with family. One of few women in both her undergraduate and graduate programs at a technological institution, Colleen describes her experiences as the only woman faculty member in her department of engineering.

Colleen O'Neal thought she wanted to be a writer, although she remembers that her high school teacher told her she was good in chemistry. While in undergraduate school, she considered dropping out many times; she persisted, primarily because she was stubborn and faced a dearth of other choices. Two teachers, one a lecturer and the other a professor with whom she did her senior thesis, had a major influence on retaining her. Both of these men took a personal interest in her progress as a student. She also finished so that she could prove to her brother that she could do it.

After obtaining her BS, she worked for 5 years at a refinery in California before returning to graduate school. After finishing graduate school at a prestigious Research I private institution in the Northeast, she obtained a faculty position at a large public Midwestern Research I institution. Desperate for money, the POWRE award made a big difference to her since it allowed her to pursue new research directions in an area in which she had not previously published. Although the men in her department ascribed to the myth that POWRE was easy to get and failed to see it as a prestigious award, it provided money for her to keep her lab going at a time when she really needed it. This proved crucial for other women in science since she had several women in her lab who eventually went into faculty positions at other institutions.

Although the climate in chemistry is better than it was when she entered the field, she is still the only woman in the department of chemical engineering. Balancing career and family has proven to be a challenge for attracting women into academic chemistry. Industry has proved that it's possible for women to have both a job and a life, but male faculty in chemistry say that women can't do the job and have a family. This deters many women who do not want to pursue the "macho" approach of being wedded to their jobs.

### Experiencing Research as an Undergraduate: Geologist Ann Edging

Persistence in the face of negative experiences also allowed Ann Edging to succeed after having a baby led to a rough start in graduate school. As she discusses in her interview, despite the length of time she has been in the department and in administration, some of Ann's faculty colleagues continue to question her commitment as a scientist because she remarried and had another child.

Ann Edging believes that the turnkey event that drew her to science was involvement in lab research early on in her undergraduate career. Because she attended the comprehensive, instead of the Research I, university in her Midwestern home state, she received plenty of attention from the faculty in the geology department. Almost immediately, she began to work with a professor on environmental impact studies. Not only did he take an interest and encourage her by providing hands-on experience with projects, but he even allowed her to run a contract that he supervised from a distance, the year he was on sabbatical.

Because undergraduate research was very important in attracting her to become a scientist, Ann incorporates working with undergraduates and devises projects with which they can evolve. She believes that without the confidence that her professor demonstrated in her as an undergraduate, she would not have persisted in science after the very negative experience she encountered when she moved to the big research university in the state for graduate school. Because she got married and had a baby, people perceived her as a "joke" who couldn't be serious about geology. After her first advisor dropped her, conversations with her undergraduate mentor provided her with the courage to seek a new advisor, who enabled her to complete her MS. She learned from this negative experience to convey positive impressions to her students about the possibilities of combining motherhood and science. She uses herself as a mother of a three-year- old and a 26-year-old as an example.

These negative graduate experiences led Ann to apply for the Ph.D. program at a major university in another state further east. Although the faculty and students at her MS-granting institution told her she would fail at her new institution, in fact she succeeded. Despite the rigor of the program and the complexity of coping with a small child, Ann believes that the absence of preconceived notions about the inability of women and mothers to become scientists allowed her to complete her Ph.D.

Immediately upon receiving her Ph.D., without taking a postdoc, she took a faculty position at a major state university in the mid-South.

She remains at the same institution today. Although the dean and upper administration have always been supportive, over the years her department has proven to be a mixed bag. Some of the older faculty, including past chairs, remained traditional and sexist, assuming that she must be more interested in marriage than field geology. At one point, she considered taking a job offered by the industry. Instead, she tried her hand at administration, serving as undergraduate director, graduate director, and eventually as associate dean for 7 years. Although she enjoyed administration, she feels that it retarded her research career, with the result that she remains an associate professor.

Currently, Ann used POWRE to refocus and reinvigorate her research program. The NSF POWRE award not only allowed her to redirect her work and to develop a track record in a different area, it also gained her new respect from her colleagues. The boost from the NSF funding and her support of two graduate students and one undergraduate are viewed positively by her colleagues. She believes that they will endorse her when she comes up for promotion to full professor in a couple of years.

## Switching Fields From Fine Arts to Computer Science: Computer Scientist Angie Verdi

Unlike all of the other scientists interviewed so far, Angie Verdi did not initially pursue science. As she reveals in her interview, art eventually led Angie to a career in computer science.

Angie Verdi knew, beginning at age 3, that she wanted to be an artist. Although she also did well in math, after high school she went to art school. Encouraged by the articles that her engineer father kept cutting out and giving her about computer graphics, she took a computer graphics course. She did well and began to talk with her instructor about going to graduate school.

While in art school she worked on animation software for PCs, which led her to work at Grummond and Davis. Her boss there talked her into going for a Ph.D. Although she began at a prestigious private institution in the metro area, her future mentor encouraged her to transfer to the Research I state university in the area. She continued to work at Grummond while pursuing her Ph.D. This complemented her academic work because she learned to write proposals and actually published her first paper before receiving her Ph.D.

Her first academic position in art and computer science at a private experimental college in the Northeast did not work out well for her. After 3 years she left for a public institution back in the metro area; this has proven to be a more suitable environment for her work. She wrote the POWRE grant to investigate a new research area her husband suggested for developing software that encourages and guides children as they work puzzles. Although the money she received from the planning grant was relatively small, it proved helpful for summer support and travel, enabling her to receive a CAREER award and other, larger grants. POWRE also led her to apply for a collaborative research experience award that supported undergraduate women.

Angie believes that juggling a family, especially during travel to conferences, becomes a major barrier for women. On-campus daycare can be a critical support, but it still doesn't solve the travel issue. Although she defines the overall climate as okay, she finds the field has low tolerance for people who have lives beyond academia. She wonders whether the pressure may be less outside of Research I institutions or if academia suits men who are content with seeing their wives only on the week-end. However, the computer science culture of acronymns and fast-paced hackers tends to be macho and intimidating to women who prefer to sit and puzzle out solutions to problems.

### Pursuing Science After Another Professional Career: Chemist Kristin Starling

Like Angie, Kristin Starling also pursued another career before she became a scientist. Not only did she take her first chemistry class at age 34, she also waited until she was in graduate school, at age 40, to have her first child.

After 11 years in a successful career as a social worker, Kristin Starling decided to pursue her love of chemistry. As an undergraduate in the late 1960s and early 1970s, she couldn't imagine being a chemist, so she majored in psychology like everyone else. She then obtained a MSW and enjoyed working as a clinical social worker.

When she married and moved to the big city with her husband, she realized that she didn't want to be a social worker in a major urban city in the Northeast. At age 34, she took her first chemistry class. Working in the engineering library at a Research I private institution she took all of the chemistry classes that she needed for application to graduate school; the staff at the lLibrary supported her pursuits, although they thought she should remain in the city for graduate school.

Her long-standing interest in environmental issues led her to a large public institution in the West, known for atmospheric chemistry. After a false start with one professor, who was an excellent scientist but had a poor track record in graduating women Ph.D.s, she switched to another research group. The head of that group was not only an outstanding scientist, but he also mentored very well. She finished her Ph.D. in 5 years, having a child at age 40, just after completing her coursework.

She remained at the same institution for an NSF-funded postdoc, although she changed labs. The equipment she devised for her environmental research now finds more use from astronomers.

She selected a comprehensive university in the West with a dual focus on teaching and research for her faculty position. As her background in social work reflects, people prove important for her, so she wanted an institution that emphasizes teaching. The particular institution Kristin chose turned out to be better in research than she anticipated, which was a pleasant surprise.

Her POWRE award has benefited her more than she realized initially. Although she wrote the grant to obtain money for two projects, she only received half of the money. She initially used that money for a device that she used in the field with her students. Results from that work made her recognize the potential for another project for which she received a second NSF grant. Success with the second project has led her to apply for a third grant to take the research in a slightly different direction.

Like many other women scientists, Kristin views herself as her own worst enemy. Because she loves research, teaching, and her family, she finds that she never has enough time to devote to all. Balancing remains a constant struggle for women scientists.

### Receiving Support From Male Colleagues: Environmental Engineer Julia Whitman

Just as a supportive male mentor and husband facilitated Kristin's success, Julia Whitman recognizes the support of her male advisor during graduate school when she had children as critical to her completion of the Ph.D. Now Julia believes that her husband's role as the stay-at-home parent, coupled with her decision to pursue a faculty position at an institution that has fewer research demands than many, has enabled her success as an engineer.

Julia Whitman can't pinpoint the early influences that made her want to become an engineer. Although neither of her parents went to college, she always wanted to be a scientist, specifically an astronaut, and her interest in the environment manifested itself as early as sixth grade when she completed a big project on the environment.

She began college as a physics major but switched to the College of Environmental Science and Forestry at a private institution in the Northeast, majoring in forest biology. After undergraduate school, she went into the Peace Corps in Kenya. After Kenya, she and her husband decided to go to graduate school at a large state institution in the Midwest. Because she did not have an undergraduate engineering degree, it took her 3 years to get her MS.

After she received her MS, she and her husband began their family. Her male advisor encouraged and supported her throughout her having children and seeking the Ph.D.; he helped her to provide some flexibility in her research timetable, allowing her to do much of her work on nights and weekends. Although she did decide that with kids the international project she wanted to pursue wasn't feasible, she became pregnant with her second child near the end of her Ph.D. research. Again her advisor was very supportive, despite her relatively slow progress. Her husband, who stopped his education after the MS, and her fellow students, all of whom were male, encouraged her.

Because she interviewed for jobs shortly after delivery, Julia had to ask to go to the bathroom to pump her breasts. She carefully selected the number of interviews and limited the places because of this constraint. Even though the department consisted of older, entrenched males, her fit with their need for a physical chemical process environmental engineer netted her an offer from a public university in New England.

The POWRE award aided Julia in making some progress in moving away from her work on water and toward a more biologically oriented project. Because of the experimental nature of her new research directions, the duration and amount of funding barely permitted her and the female students with whom she is committed to working to initiate the project.

Julia believes that the expectation that scientists and engineers will work all hours and travel extensively becomes the biggest barrier for women. This expectation makes it difficult to have a balanced family life, and most women do not have a stay-at-home spouse the way many men do. Her husband runs the farm and takes care of their children, but it's still difficult, even though her university does not make the research demands required by many institutions. Since most women don't want to give up having a family, they drop out of science and do not pursue administrative positions that demand long hours and considerable travel.

The removal of the blatant sexism and discrimination in engineering has not resulted in eradication of subtle, undermining behaviors in the workplace. The influx of large numbers of male engineers from foreign countries into the profession has also made life more difficult for the women. For example, when a colleague of hers got divorced, the Muslim male engineer with whom she worked refused to speak with her. Some of these men expect the women to defer to them and refuse to collaborate with them on projects. Although women engineers have difficulty verbalizing the problems, the climate makes them feel isolated, underappreciated, and constantly undermined.

## Adapting Successfully to a New Country: Computer Scientist Marina Titelinska

As a foreign-born scientist herself, Marina Titelinska also viewed her husband's support, which differed substantially from that received by Kristin and Julia from their spouses, as significant for her success as a scientist. Although she arranged her career to coincide with his geographic moves, including from Poland to North American, her husband has often given Marina ideas and advice useful to her as a computer scientist.

Marina Titelinska started her family at age 20 while she was still an undergraduate student in Poland. She also completed her first MS degree in electrical engineering and worked for a short period while her husband completed his Ph.D. Following him to a private university in Canada, she made the transition from EE to computer science, working in computational geometry for 1 year.

Her husband then moved to a state Research I university in the Northeast, where he remains today. Although no one there worked in computational geometry, Marina received her MS in computer science and began work on her Ph.D. She had an unpleasant experience with her advisor who came from Persia and for whom she was his first Ph.D student. Because he wanted to control her, they fought over many issues, including publication of papers. She also managed to undertake 2 years of work at the prestigious public university in the neighboring state, working with a famous researcher on robotics.

She credits both of her parents who were biochemists for inspiring her to finish, since they raised her to finish what she started. Marina completed her Ph.D, while accompanying her husband on his sabbatical in California, at the same time that she gave birth to her second son.

Although she obtained a faculty position at a private Northeastern institution, she realized that few people, especially women, received tenure there. Two years later she began to have contacts with the medical school, through a wonderful woman vice president who developed the "visible human project," at a private Research I university in the metro area. Working to develop software in medical imaging and computer graphics merged her current with her original interests.

The POWRE award helped Marina bridge to the private Research I institution because it provided her with amazing freedom to establish a new project. She applied for a big collaborative grant, which became one of the first to introduce computer science techniques into the medical school. She remains happy there.

Although she and her husband have never collaborated as scientists, he has often given her ideas and advice. Both came from academic families, and he has been tough on her, but supportive. She believes that their forties are proving to be the best time of their lives for both career and family. Their sons are now 12 and 22.

Marina attempts to attract and retain other women in math and physical sciences. Her life demonstrates the possibility of combining a Ph.D. in computer science with being a wife and mother. She still coadvises a student from her former institution who has three kids and is the first in her family to receive any college degree. She tries to advise the daughters of her friends who show an interest in math and science.

Marina thinks that in the United States the difficulty of coping with kids while having an academic career becomes a major barrier for women. Better daycare would help tremendously. However, she believes that the overriding concern for all scientists in the U.S. is that academia is not valued, despite the excellent system of higher education. The U.S. public views neither scientists nor academia as prestigious. With additional barriers for women, why would American women choose academic science or engineering?

## Using Institutional Constraints to Move to a Better Situation: Biologist Jeannette Oatson

Like Marina, Jeannette Oatson also left her country of origin and family in England to pursue her scientific career in North America. In a pattern similar to that of Marina, Jeannette first worked in Canada before coming to the United States, where she has had a long, successful academic career as both a biologist and an administrator.

Jeannette Oatson was born in the mid-1950s in England. Although both of her parents had left school at age 14, she benefited from the educational reform that swept England after World War II. Because of her excellent score on the 11+ exam, she entered an exclusive girls school, that had been private until about a decade earlier. In this all-female environment, she failed to develop the conception that men did science and women didn't.

Unable to attend Cambridge or Oxford, she went to a British university that was very strong in science and engineering. Unaware of career choices, she refused offers to go into medicine, believing she should teach grammar school, a career she saw as more compatible with being a wife and mother. In her final year, the faculty told Jeannette that if she completed a first-class degree, they would give her a scholarship for the Ph.D. The independent research project she pursued as an undergraduate not only helped her to be one of five her class of 100 receiving a first-class degree, it also hooked her into research.

When she completed her Ph.D. in 1984 at the age of 24, it coincided with Margaret Thatcher's reforms of the British educational system, which resulted in a huge brain drain. Jeannette took a postdoc at a Canadian institution in one of the western provinces. After three and a half years as a postdoc, she decided to stay in North America, preferably Canada. Ultimately, she landed at a large public Research I institution in the Southeastern U.S. in zoology. The paternalistic environment there made it difficult for women. Married after she achieved tenure, one of her colleagues asked her if one child wasn't enough when she became pregnant again, this time with twins. Although she did make full professor within 10 years, she was not put up for early promotion as was the young male whose record trailed hers. She felt that the chair and dean did not care about the situation for women.

In 1994, she took the position as chair of the department at a comprehensive Midwestern state institution. Now a dean, she has enjoyed her time in the Midwest and the institutional opportunities available. The POWRE award came at a critical time, as she attempted to move from systems to cellular and molecular techniques. It also coincided with her move to the Midwest and facilitated the transfer.

As she ages, Jeannette becomes demoralized when she realizes that women continue to be marginalized and isolated. Although she has fought hard for the younger women and has some power to do that now that she has administrative positions, she finds the overall climate as bad or worse than when she struggled as a graduate student and assistant professor. She sees the battlefield strewn with casualties of women who leave science, become dissuaded, or fail to achieve the respect they deserve.

### Working Before Pursuing Higher Education: Computer Scientist Joan Frain

Although Angie and Kristin did not pursue science as their initial careers, they did go to college immediately after high school. In contrast, Joan Frain worked for 5 years before beginning computer science classes at a junior college. In her interview, Joan describes a nontraditional career path that serves as a role model for women in computer science who wonder if it's possible to balance career and family.

Joan Frain did not enter college immediately after high school; instead she began to major in computer science 5 years later at a junior college. She decided to go into pure math and computer science in the mid-South. Upon graduation, she worked in the industry as a programmer and software engineer.

Highly motivated to continue her education when she moved to the East Coast with her husband, she entered a private Research I urban university and pursued an MS in computer science. Although she looked for a job, she began to feel that she didn't know enough, so she entered a state university. After three years, just as she passed her qualifying exams, her husband lost his job. She followed him to a large metropolitan area in the Southeast and found a professor in computing who took an interest in her work, after she showed him a paper she was writing. He gave her a research assistantship, a desk, and more important, motivated her to work hard. After 3 years there, she finished her Ph.D. from the Northeastern state university and stayed on at the Southeastern institution for a postdoc, working with the same professor in the Southeast who supported her in graduate school.

The POWRE award proved critical for letting her pull away and distance herself from her faculty mentor in the Southeast to build her own career. It permitted her to obtain several publications and the right to say "no" to continuing to run his research. The NSF award also looked good on her curriculum vitae.

Although at the time she held the POWRE award, she did not have a position from which she could help other women; now, as an

assistant professor at a public Midwestern research I institution, Joan
has several women students. She believes that culture stands as the
primary barrier for women in computer science. Many women interested in computer science have a creative, artistic bent. They perceive
that they don't fit in to the hacker, nerd culture.

In addition to family friendly policies such as having a daycare
center on campus, having a senior woman as a department head can
make a tremendous difference in attracting women and modifying
the behavior of senior men. Because the numbers of women majoring
in computer science are dropping so rapidly, the presence of other
women is especially critical.

### Using Design to Combine Arts and Engineering: Civil Engineer Pat Pearson

A liberal arts college in the South allowed Pat Pearson to combine her
love of art and art history with technology in a very different way from
computer scientist Angie Verdi. Pat Pearson is a civil engineer special-
izing in concrete technology:

> Pat Pearson grew up in a traditional family, with a physician father
> and a mother who worked as his receptionist. Her divorced aunt, a
> Ph.D. recipient from a prestigious technical institution, who works as
> a consultant in the Northeast serves as her role model.
>
> Although Pat entered a private Southern institution with an equal
> interest in art history and engineering, she pursued engineering
> because of the scholarship she received. The small classes allowed her
> to receive significant attention from mentors who encouraged her and
> invited her to pursue research while an undergraduate. She particu-
> larly credits one professor, an MIT Ph.D., who encouraged her to
> compete in graduate school. In graduate school at the large public
> Research I on the West Coast, her interest in design led her to spe-
> cialize in concrete technology, realizing that design influences peo-
> ple's behavior.
>
> She followed the wishes of her husband, who was 2 years behind
> her in the program because he had worked for a while in industry,
> and took a faculty position in a very good place so that they could
> maximize their opportunities as a couple. Although she might have
> preferred a smaller liberal arts college or less prestigious institution,

she took the position in civil engineering at a Research I institute public institution in the South. This opened the door for her husband to take a faculty position there in the department rated number one in the country in his field. Sometimes she wishes for a less high-pressure situation, particularly since now, at age 30 and in her third year on the faculty, they are considering starting a family.

The POWRE grant provided Pat with the opportunity to get started on her research. She used it as a springboard for other funding. She also supported one male and three female students with the grant.

Although Pat views balancing career and family as the greatest obstacle for women engineers, she recognizes other issues surrounding access to facilities and recruitment of students. She also notes the visibility of women in a field in which they are an extreme minority. This can be advantageous, since if they do well they will be remembered. However, mistakes are equally evident and memorable.

## Conclusion

The family backgrounds, educational experiences, peer and faculty influences, and personal circumstances of each of these 11 women combines to make each woman's career path as a scientist or engineer unique. Some, such as Angie Verdi and Marina Titelinska, received encouragement and guidance to go into science from parents who were scientists or engineers themselves. In contrast, Julia Whitman and Jeannette Oatson had parents who had not gone to college, but who supported their daughters in their interest in science. Although most knew from an early age that they desired a career in science, Angie Verdi and Pat Pearson pursued an initial interest in art or art history. Some such as Jeannette Oatson and Marina Titelinska left their country of birth to pursue science in the United States, while Suzanne Hausmann and Julia Whitman found that time spent in Europe and Africa helped to strengthen and define their interest in a particular field of science or engineering.

Although most of the women interviewed entered an undergraduate major in science immediately after high school, Joan Frain entered junior college 5 years later; Kristin Starling began to study chemistry at age 34, after 11 years in a successful career as a social worker. Most had someone who encouraged or mentored them along the way, although many of those mentors were male, with some from outside academia. Most who had children became pregnant while in graduate school, but Jeannette Oatson waited until she achieved tenure. Although all interviewees hold faculty positions in Research I or comprehensive institutions that vary in the emphasis placed on the balance between research and teaching, the women hold different ranks ranging from assistant (Jane Fields) through associate (Ann Edging) to full professor (Jeannette Oatson). Both Ann Edging and Jeannette Oatson have tried their hand at academic administration.

The stories of the 11 women POWRE awardees interviewed for this chapter underline the unique pathway and set of experiences of each individual's career in science or engineering. They reveal that no stereotype defines these women and that no magic key or career manual reveals the guideposts along their journey that brought them to this career point.

Despite their differences, these women are united in their ability to put together a combination of decisions about family and profession that have enabled them to pursue a successful academic career. Careful reading of these stories, coupled with the quantitative responses of almost 400 women to the e-mail questionnaire presented in the next chapter, reveals that women scientists and engineers also express similar difficulties with institutional policies and structure that undercut their love of science and engineering.

# CHAPTER 2
## OPPORTUNITIES AND CHALLENGES

Almost 60 years ago, Dr. Vannevar Bush, the de facto science advisor of President Franklin D. Roosevelt, responded to the president's request for advice on how the lessons learned from the World War II organization of science and engineering could be applied in peacetime (National Science Board, 2000). Bush's 1945 report — "Science: The Endless Frontier" — became the blueprint for the long-term U.S. national investment in scientific research and education through research universities, industry, and government that led to the establishment of the National Science Foundation (NSF). Almost four decades later, the Science and Technology Equal Opportunities Act of 1980 mandated that the NSF collect and analyze data and report to Congress on a biennial basis on the status of women and minorities in the science and engineering professions. In 1982, NSF published the first congressionally mandated reports documenting trends in the participation of women and minorities in science and engineering. These biennial reports on Women and Minorities in Science and Engineering, to which Persons with Disabilities were added in 1984, provided the data documenting that science and engineering have lower representation of men of color and women compared to their proportions in the U.S. population overall (NSF, 2000, p. xii).

**Women's Programs at NSF in the 1980s**

These reports laid the statistical foundation for NSF officials to plan program initiatives to address these underrepresentations. Programs such as Research Opportunities for Women and Visiting Professorships for Women (VPW) exemplify these initiatives. As Mary Clutter recounted in the evaluation of POWRE conference in 1998 (Rosser & Zieseniss, 1998), the director of NSF established a task force on programs for women in the spring of 1989 with the following charge:

> to review the existing Foundation programs aimed at women in science and engineering, ascertain the barriers to women's full participation in science and engineering, and recommend changes in the Foundation's programs promoting such full participation, as well as an overall strategic plan for the National Science Foundation in this area. (Clutter, 1998, Appendix B)

The task force concluded the following:

1. significant progress has been made in increasing the representation of women in the sciences
2. there are serious problems remaining preventing the recruitment, retention and advancement of women in science and engineering, and
3. these problems are more severe in some fields than in others, although advancement to senior ranks is a problem in all fields. (Clutter, 1998, Appendix B)

The task force also made several specific recommendations, including expanding the level of effort in some existing programs at intervention points along the pipeline and establishing two new programs: one designed to enhance the graduate environment in academic institutions; the second designed to recognize and advance outstanding women faculty to the senior ranks (Clutter, 1998, Appendix B).

The NSF funded several initiatives targeted toward various segments of the science and engineering pipeline. Graduate Fellowships for Women provided an incentive for women graduate students to remain in graduate school and complete their Ph.D. These fellowships provided support for individual women and their individual research in science and engineering.

Career Advancement Awards (CAA), initiated in 1986, were superseded by Professional Opportunities for Women in Research and Education (POWRE) in fiscal year 1998. As the CAA name suggests, the award focused on advancing the careers of individual women by providing funds to pursue their own research agenda. By targeting junior women, CAA used a combination of release from teaching and recognition of potential to make a significant research contribution, to place these women on a fast track to academic success in science or engineering research.

The task force also recommended that the NSF "Incorporate the existing Research Opportunities for Women programs into Division-level strategic plans, but retain the Visiting Professorship as a Foundation-wide program" (Clutter, 1998, Appendix B). Most NSF program officers have funds to support Research Planning Grants, which provide money for small-scale or pilot projects that serve as a prelude to a larger grant for the bigger, more complex research project that will be undertaken eventually. Many of the divisions used a segment of the Research Planning Grant funds as discretionary add-ons, often called Research Planning Grants for Women. These grants supported the research projects of individual women and particularly targeted women scientists or engineers who had never held an NSF grant or who sought reentry after a career interruption.

VPW initially established in late 1982 (SRI International, 1994), stood as the primary, cross-directorate initiative to retain women that remained foundation-wide after the 1989 task force report until POWRE succeeded it in fiscal year 1997. VPW sought to retain women who already had faculty appointments in science and engineering and to provide them with research opportunities and exposure to further their careers. The primary thrust of VPW underwrote the research goals and projects of individual women scientists. VPW facilitated women's exposure to new equipment, new approaches, and the different environment of another institution as a mechanism to boost their research and/or provide new exposure. A 1994 evaluation of VPW was very positive toward the program and documented that a "VPW award comes at a critical time for keeping the recipient active in research as opposed to other academic, non-research responsibilities" (p. 13).

Although support of research of individual women scientists and engineers served as the predominant focus for the VPW during most of its 14-year history, each VPW was required to spend approximately 30% of her time and effort to attract and retain women scientists and engineers at the institutions they were visiting (SRI International, 1994). As part of their "interactive activities that involve teaching, mentoring, and other student contacts," VPWs engaged in activities such as forming the Society of Women Engineers (SWE) chapters, establishing mentor networks among women graduate students, and teaching women in science courses jointly with women's studies programs (p. 1). This division of 70% support for individual research and 30% to improve the infrastructure to attract and retain women in science and engineering signaled a recognition that support of individual research alone might not be sufficient to increase the numbers and percentages of women scientists and engineers. The 30% underlined the dawning realization that steps needed to be taken at the institutional, as well as individual, levels.

### Women's Programs in the Early 1990s

Although Faculty Awards for Women (FAW) held only one program solicitation, in 1990, FAW attempted to address a systemic problem—the dearth of women scientists and engineers in senior positions that the task force report had identified. The initiative used the traditional approach of supporting the research projects, for a period of 5 years at the level of $50,000 per year, of individual women faculty in its attempt to solve the systemic problem. Almost all of the 100 awardees achieved the primary stated goal of the program of achieving tenure. The controversy within the peer review panel surrounding the criteria for selection of the FAW awardees (reviewers could not come to a consensus over whether individuals who showed potential, but appeared to need a boost, or those whose records indicated they were very likely to receive tenure even without the award, should receive higher priority) contributed to the termination of the program after 1 year. It was difficult to judge the efficacy of this program of support for research of individual investigators as an approach to systemic change, given that there was only one cohort of awardees.

Recognizing that a focus on efforts to target individuals in groups such as minorities and White women would not work as long as the system remained unchanged, the directorate of education and human resources at NSF began to focus on systemic initiatives. In addition to Statewide Systemic Initiatives (SSI), Urban Systemic Initiatives (USI), and Rural Systemic Initiatives (RSI), the NSF established the Program for Women and Girls (PWG) in 1993 to explore comprehensive factors and climate issues that may systematically deter women from science and engineering. In addition to dissemination projects, PWG included two other initiatives for women and girls: Model Projects for Women and Girls (MPWG) encouraged "the design, implementation, evaluation and dissemination of innovative, short-term highly focused activities which will improve the access to and/or retention of females in SEM (science, engineering, and mathematics) education and careers" (NSF, 1993, p. 7), and Experimental Projects for Women and Girls (EPWG) which encompassed large-scale projects requiring a consortial effort with multiple target populations. They aimed "to create positive and permanent changes in academic, social, and scientific climates (for classrooms, laboratories, departments, institutions/organizations) in order to allow the interest and aptitude women and girls display in SEM to flourish; and to add to the knowledge base about interactions between gender and the infrastructure of SEM which can provide direction for future efforts" (NSF, 1993, p. 7).

The only individual research projects supported under the PWG were those where the research and evaluation of a curricular change, cocurricular program, or faculty development initiative fit the individual researcher's agenda. Although K–12 always constituted the centerpiece of PWG, undergraduates, graduate students, and even faculty served as primary targets of several projects at the beginning of PWG. After 1995–96, and particularly after VPW was incorporated into PWG in late 1995, eventually to be succeeded by the cross-directorate POWRE, PWG centered on K–16 exclusively. Reincarnated as the Program for Gender Equity, the program solicitation stated the following under goals:

Research
- To discover and describe gender-based differences and preferences in learning science and mathematics, K–16
- To discover and describe barriers to female students' interest and performance in science and mathematics
- To increase the knowledge of organizational models that lead to more equitable and inviting SMET educational environments, K–16
- To increase national research capacity in the field of gender and SMET education by developing new researchers and research-oriented education practitioners. (NSF, 2001a, pp. 7–8)

Although the PGE was retitled Gender Diversity in Science, Technology, Engineering and Mathematics Education (GDSE) in 2002–03, the focus on K–16 has continued as this volume goes to press (NSF, 2003).

*Initiatives in the Late 1990s: Origins of POWRE*
After the 1996 VPW solicitation, NSF replaced VPW with Professional Opportunities for Women in Research and Education (POWRE), with the first POWRE awards distributed in fiscal year 1997. POWRE was conceived in the wake of the November 1994 Republican sweep of Congress, where 62% of White males voted Republican (Edsall, 1995). This resulted in cuts in federal spending, with programs that had gender and/or race as their central focus under particular scrutiny. In response to statements suggesting that Republican lawmakers were studying whether federal affirmative action requirements should be dropped on the grounds that they discriminate against White men (made by Senate Majority Leader Robert Dole on NBC's *Meet the Press* on February 5, 1995), President Clinton initiated his own review of affirmative action programs (Swoboda, 1995, p. A1). In June 1995, the U.S. Supreme Court ruled in the *Adarand Constructors, Inc. v Pena* decision that "federal affirmative action programs that use racial and ethnic criteria as a basis for decision making are subject to strict judicial scrutiny" (in Kole, 1995, p. 1). On July 19, after holding a press conference to reaffirm his commitment to affirmative action, President Clinton issued a memorandum for heads of executive

departments and agencies to bring them in line with the Supreme Court decision. On July 20, 1995, the University of California Board of Regents voted to end special admissions programs; that decision was confirmed a year later by a citizen referendum. In 1996, a Texas circuit court ruling banned affirmative action in admissions and financial awards. In 1998, in a referendum, the citizens of the state of Washington prohibited any "preferential treatment on the basis of race, gender, national origin, or ethnicity." In July 2000, an administrative judge upheld Florida Governor Jeb Bush's plan to end the consideration of race and gender in admissions in state colleges in his state (Lauer, 2000). The Supreme Court's decision on the University of Michigan's case on affirmative action occurred after POWRE ended in 2001, so discussion of its impact is not included here.

Although the NSF initiatives challenged in court focused on minority programs, specifically the Summer Science Camps and the Graduate Minority Fellowships, programs targeted exclusively for women principal investigators such as VPW, FAW, CAA were thought to be in jeopardy. Since the MPWG and EPWG had some men as PIs and did not exclude boys and men from projects, while targeting girls and women, PWG was considered safe, with the exception of VPW.

Since VPW had moved to PWG only in 1995, POWRE replaced it after the 1996 solicitation; CAA and RPG were subsumed by POWRE in fiscal year 1998. Rather than being housed in education and human resources where PWG, VPW, FAW, CAA had been housed, POWRE became a cross-directorate program, created with the following objectives:

- To provide opportunities for further career advancement, professional growth, and increased prominence of women in engineering and in the disciplines of science supported by NSF.
- To encourage more women to pursue careers in science and engineering by providing greater visibility for women scientists and engineers in academic institutions and in industry. (NSF, 1997, p. 1)

Despite threats against affirmative action, the approach to achieving these objectives came through individual grants to support science and engineering research of individual women researchers. POWRE did not retain from VPW the concept of committing 30% of time devoted to infrastructure to attract and retain women in science and engineering.

NSF became aware of several factors that might mitigate against POWRE and its effectiveness almost immediately:

1.  The request for proposals for POWRE had been put together very rapidly.

2.  POWRE had been removed from the former site of VPW (EHR and HRD) because PWG was focusing increasingly on K–12; this meant that program officers from the research directorates, rather than from the PWG, were overseeing POWRE.

3.  Moving POWRE to the research directorates, coupled with having 100% of the time and support going to the science and engineering research of individual investigators, went against a growing sentiment that support for institutional and systemic approaches, rather than support of the research of individual women scientists, would be required to increase the percentage of women at all levels in science and engineering.

In response to these and a variety of other factors, NSF decided to organize a workshop of NSF program directors and scientists and engineers from the professional community to study POWRE and provide recommendations. Included in the recommendations emerging from the workshop were the following:

> Participants in the POWRE Workshop believe that NSF has a much greater opportunity for enabling women scientists in research and education that goes beyond the program POWRE. We suggest that this opportunity be addressed with a series of longer term strategies that fall outside the parameters of POWRE, as well as through POWRE. In keeping with its combined focus on research and education, NSF should develop long-term strategies to encourage institutional transformation regarding the culture of science and to increase gender and ethnic diversity among scientists for both faculty and students; targeted programs such as POWRE do not have sufficient resources to bring about institutional change, which must also be

encouraged by all programs in each directorate. The short-term individual strategies, through POWRE, should facilitate women to participate fully in all of NSF's programs, with an aim of developing institutions into places where women scientists and engineers can succeed as well as men. Grants to individuals or to groups of investigators should be made with this goal in mind, as well as the goal of helping the grant recipients' careers. (Rosser & Zieseniss, 1998, p. 9)

This recommendation foreshadows the ADVANCE initiative in its acknowledgment of the need for "long-term strategies to encourage institutional transformation." It also underlines the insufficiency of POWRE and its approach of funding research of individual investigators to bring about structural changes needed to increase the numbers of women scientists and engineers.

## Methods of Analyzing THE POWRE Survey

As part of the preparation for the workshop, I sent a brief e-mail questionnaire survey to the POWRE awardees for fiscal year 1997. The results of that questionnaire proved to be more than useful for the workshop. They provided such interesting insights about the lives of women scientists and engineers that I decided to continue the survey during all 4 years of the POWRE program. All POWRE new grant awardees for fiscal years 1997, 1998, 1999, and 2000 were sent a questionnaire via e-mail. The questionnaire included the following two questions:

1. What are the most significant issues/challenges/opportunities facing women scientists today as they plan their careers?
2. How does the laboratory climate (or its equivalent in your subdiscipline) impact upon the careers of women scientists?

Response rates for the e-mail survey were as follows: 71.6% of the 1997 awardees, 76.6% of the 1998 awardees, 65.5% of the 1999 awardees, and 63.5% of the 2000 awardees. Table 4 shows that the women receiving POWRE awards in all 4 years represented all directorates of NSF disciplines. The success rate (percentage of applicants receiving funding) ranged from 12% to 47% among the seven directorates, and the overall success rate increased from 19% in 1997, 25% in 1998, 27%

in 1999, to 33% in 2000. These success rates underline the extremely competitive nature of POWRE, since only one in five proposals received funding in the first year, and only one-third were funded in the final year. The 33% rate reached parity with other NSF programs at the time, indicating that contrary to the myths circulating about the initiative, POWRE was equally or more competitive than most NSF initiatives.

Sixty-seven of the 96 POWRE awardees for fiscal year 1997, 119 of the 173 awardees for fiscal year 1998, 98 of the 159 fiscal year 1999 awardees, and 105 of the 170 fiscal year 2000 awardees to whom the e-mail survey was sent responded. The nonresponse rate ranged between 23% and 37% over the 4-year period; some failures to respond were the result of invalid e-mail addresses. In addition to failures to respond, life circumstances prevented acceptance of the award in some cases. For example, in fiscal year 2000, one awardee was killed in an accident, and one responded that personal circumstances surrounding a divorce postponed her acceptance of the award.

As Table 5 shows, the sample responding to the e-mail questionnaire in all four years appeared to be representative of the population of awardees with regard to discipline, and the non-respondents did not appear to cluster in a particular discipline. The limited data available from the e-mail responses revealed no other respondent or non-respondent bias (Rosser, 2001). The relatively large sample size coupled with lack of disciplinary bias suggests that these data might be generalized to the broader population of women scientists and engineers, particularly at Research I and comprehensive institutions.

### Results

Question 1: What are the most significant issues/challenges/opportunities facing women scientists today as they plan their careers? (see Table 6)

The details of the procedure used to develop the 16 basic categories for responses to question 1 have been previously published for fiscal year 1997 awardees (see Rosser & Zieseniss, 2000). The categories emerged from my coding of the textual replies. The four categories in Table 7

**TABLE 4** Summary Information for POWRE Awards for FY 1997, 1998, 1999, 2000

| DIRECTOR-ATE OR OFFICE[a] | FY97 SUBMITTED POWRE PROPOSALS | TOTAL FY97 GRANTS[c] | FY97 OVERALL SUCCESS RATE % | FY98 SUBMITTED POWRE PROPOSALS | TOTAL FY98 GRANTS[c] | FY98 OVERALL SUCCESS RATE % | FY99 SUBMITTED POWRE PROPOSALS | TOTAL FY99 GRANTS | FY99 OVERALL SUCCESS RATE % | FY00 SUBMITTED POWRE PROPOSALS | TOTAL FY00 GRANTS | FY00 OVERALL SUCCESS RATE % |
|---|---|---|---|---|---|---|---|---|---|---|---|---|
| BIO | 142 | 17 | 12 | 214 | 43 | 20 | 159 | 36 | 23 | 144 | 41 | 28 |
| CISE | 50 | 10 | 20 | 63 | 19 | 30 | 43 | 10 | 23 | 36 | 11 | 31 |
| EHR | 12 | 3 | 25 | 25 | 7 | 28 | 32 | 7 | 22 | 24 | 6 | 25 |
| ENG | 90 | 19 | 21 | 118 | 28 | 24 | 119 | 30 | 25 | 94 | 26 | 28 |
| GEO | 51 | 10 | 20 | 59 | 15 | 25 | 50 | 12 | 24 | 42 | 17 | 40 |
| MPS | 100 | 18 | 18 | 118 | 34 | 29 | 110 | 43 | 39 | 94 | 44 | 47 |
| SBE | 59 | 19 | 32 | 104 | 27 | 26 | 70 | 21 | 30 | 85 | 25 | 29 |
| Totals[b] | 504 | 96 | 19 | 701 | 173 | 25 | 583 | 159 | 27 | 519 | 170 | 33 |

[a]The NSF directorates represented in this study include Biological Sciences (BIO); Computer and Information Science and Engineering (CISE); Education and Human Resources (EHR); Engineering (ENG); Geosciences (GEO); Mathematical and Physical Sciences (MPS); and Social, Behavioral, and Economic Sciences (SBE).

[b]This analysis does not include three respondents from the OPP directorate for FY97 and FY98 because the total number of respondents was too small to provide meaningful information. Therefore, the totals in this table for each award year do not include the OPP awards.

[c]Some directorates included supplemental grants in their total grants awarded.

**TABLE 5** Numbers and Disciplinary Distribution of Respondents to Questionnaire

| NSF DIRECTORATE OR OFFICE[a] | TOTAL FY97 GRANTS[b] | RESPONDED TO E-MAIL QUESTIONS | TOTAL FY98 GRANTS[b] | RESPONDED TO E-MAIL QUESTIONS | TOTAL FY99 GRANTS | RESPONDED TO E-MAIL QUESTIONS | TOTAL FY00 GRANTS | RESPONDED TO E-MAIL QUESTIONS |
|---|---|---|---|---|---|---|---|---|
| BIO | 17 | 10 | 43 | 27 | 36 | 25 | 41 | 22 |
| CISE | 10 | 10 | 19 | 11 | 10 | 6 | 11 | 8 |
| EHR | 3 | 3 | 7 | 1 | 7 | 5 | 6 | 3 |
| ENG | 19 | 15 | 28 | 23 | 30 | 18 | 26 | 13 |
| GEO | 10 | 8 | 15 | 10 | 12 | 8 | 17 | 12 |
| MPS | 18 | 9 | 34 | 22 | 43 | 25 | 44 | 28 |
| SBE | 19 | 12 | 27 | 22 | 21 | 11 | 25 | 18 |
| Unknown[d] | n/a | — | n/a | 3[c] | n/a | — | n/a | 1[c] |
| Totals[d] | 96 | 67 | 173 | 119[e] | 159 | 98[f] | 170 | 105 |

[a] The NSF directorates represented in this study include Biological Sciences (BIO); Computer and Information Science and Engineering (CISE); Education and Human Resources (EHR); Engineering (ENG); Geosciences (GEO); Mathematical and Physical Sciences (MPS); and Social, Behavioral, and Economic Sciences (SBE).

[b] Some directorates included supplemental grants in their total grants awarded.

[c] For three FY98 respondents and one FY00 respondent, the directorate was not evident from the e-mail address.

[d] This analysis does not include three respondents from the OPP directorate for FY97 and FY98 because the total number of respondents was too small to provide meaningful information. Therefore the totals in this table for each award year do not include the OPP awards.

[e] Three unknown directorates and five late respondents, not included in previous analyses (see Rosser, 2001), were included in this analysis.

[f] One additional respondent, not available in a prior study (Rosser, 2001) was added to the FY99 data for this analysis.

represent groupings of more similar responses that emerged from a discussion of the 16 categories and data at a national conference by 30 social scientists, scientists, and engineers whose work focuses on women and science (Rosser, 1999). The same codes and categories were applied to the responses from fiscal-year 1998, 1999, and 2000 awardees. Although most respondents replied with more than one answer, in some years at least one awardee gave no answer to the question. While the survey data are categorical and therefore not appropriate for means testing, differences in responses across award years and across directorates clearly emerge when response frequencies are examined.

As Table 6 shows, overwhelming numbers of respondents across all 4 years found balancing work with family (response 1) to be the most significant challenge facing women scientists and engineers. During all 4 years, large percentages of respondents ranked time management issues (response 2), isolation and lack of camaraderie, mentoring due to small numbers (response 3), gaining credibility and respectability from peers (response 4), and two career placements (response 5) as major challenges. Time management (response 2) appeared to be less of a problem; whereas affirmative action/backlash/discrimination (response 9) seemed to be more of a problem for 1998, 1999, and 2000 awardees. Fiscal year 2000 awardees reported low numbers of women (response 3) and positive responses (response 10) at higher rates than awardees in previous years.

Table 7 shows the grouping of the responses to question 1 into four categories. Adding restrictions because of spousal situations (responses 5 and 7) to balancing work with family responsibilities (response 1) suggests that category A — pressures women face in balancing career and family — is the most significant barrier identified by women scientists and engineers regardless of directorate or year of award. A second grouping (responses 3, 4, 8, 10, and 12) appears to result from the low numbers of women scientists and engineers and consequent stereotypes surrounding expectations about their performance. Isolation and lack of mentoring as well as gaining credibility and respectability from peers and administrators typify category B. Category C (responses 2, 6, and 16) includes issues faced by both men and women scientists and engineers in the current environment of tight resources that may pose

**TABLE 6** Total Responses to Question 1

### Question 1: What are the most significant issues/challenges/opportunities facing women scientists today as they plan their careers?

| | CATEGORIES | 1997 % OF RESPONSES | | 1998 % OF RESPONSES | | 1999 % OF RESPONSES | | 2000 % OF RESPONSES | |
|---|---|---|---|---|---|---|---|---|---|
| 1 | Balancing work with family responsibilities (children, elderly relatives, etc.) | 62.7 | (42/67) | 72.3 | (86/119) | 77.6 | (76/98) | 71.4 | (75/105) |
| 2 | Time management/balancing committee responsibilities with research and teaching | 22.4 | (15/67) | 10.1 | (12/119) | 13.3 | (13/98) | 13.3 | (14/105) |
| 3 | Low numbers of women, isolation and lack of camaraderie/mentoring | 23.9 | (16/67) | 18.5 | (22/119) | 18.4 | (18/98) | 30.5 | (33/105) |
| 4 | Gaining credibility/respectability from peers and administrators | 22.4 | (15/67) | 17.6 | (21/119) | 19.4 | (19/98) | 21.9 | (23/105) |
| 5 | "Two career" problem (balance with spouse's career) | 23.9 | (16/67) | 10.9 | (13/119) | 20.4 | (20/98) | 20.0 | (21/105) |
| 6 | Lack of funding/inability to get funding | 7.5 | (5/67) | 4.2 | (5/119) | 10.2 | (10/98) | 8.6 | (9/105) |
| 7 | Job restrictions (location, salaries, etc.) | 9.0 | (6/67) | 9.2 | (11/119) | 7.1 | (7/98) | 5.7 | (6/105) |
| 8 | Networking | 6.0 | (4/67) | <1 | (1/119) | 0 | (0/98) | 4.8 | (5/105) |
| 9 | Affirmative action backlash/discrimination | 6.0 | (4/67) | 15.1 | (18/119) | 14.3 | (14/98) | 12.4 | (13/105) |
| 10 | Positive: active recruitment of women/more opportunities | 6.0 | (4/67) | 10.1 | (12/119) | 9.2 | (9/98) | 14.3 | (15/105) |
| 11 | Establishing independence | 3.0 | (2/67) | 0 | (0/119) | 6.1 | (6/98) | 2.9 | (3/105) |
| 12 | Negative social images | 3.0 | (2/67) | 3.4 | (4/119) | 2.0 | (2/98) | <1 | (1/105) |
| 13 | Trouble gaining access to nonacademic positions | 1.5 | (1/67) | 1.7 | (2/119) | 1.0 | (1/98) | 1.9 | (2/105) |
| 14 | Sexual harassment | 1.5 | (1/67) | <1 | (1/119) | 2.0 | (2/98) | 1.9 | (2/105) |
| 15 | No answer | 0 | (0/67) | <1 | (1/119) | 1.0 | (1/98) | 1.9 | (2/105) |
| 16 | Cut-throat competition | -- | -- | -- | -- | 1.0 | (1/98) | 1.9 | (2/105) |

**TABLE 7** Categorization of Question 1 Across Year of Award

**Question 1: What are the most significant issues/challenges/opportunities facing women scientists today as they plan their careers?**

| CATEGORIES | RESPONSE NUMBERS[a,c] | MEANS OF RESPONSES % | | | |
| --- | --- | --- | --- | --- | --- |
| | | 1997 | 1998 | 1999 | 2000 |
| A  Pressures women face in balancing career and family | 1, 5, 7 | 31.9 | 30.8 | 35.0 | 32.4 |
| B[b] Problems faced by women because of their low numbers and stereotypes held by others regarding gender | 3, 4, 8, 10, 12 | 12.3 | 10.1 | 9.8 | 14.5 |
| C[b] Issues faced by both men and women scientists and engineers in the current environment of tight resources, which may pose particular difficulties for women | 2, 6, 16 | 10.0 | 4.8 | 8.2 | 7.9 |
| D  More overt discrimination and harassment | 9, 11, 13, 14 | 3.0 | 4.4 | 5.8 | 4.8 |

[a] Given the responses from all 4 years, after receiving faculty comments at various presentations of this research, and after working with the data, we exchanged two questions from categories B and D to better reflect the response groupings. Specifically, responses 10 and 12 (considered in category D in Rosser & Zieseniss, 2000) were moved to category B. Similarly, responses 11 and 13 (included in category B in Rosser and Zieseniss, 2000) were placed in category D.
[b] The alphabetic designation for categories B and C have been exchanged, compared with earlier papers (Rosser & Zieseniss, 2000) to present descending response percentages.
[c] Response 15 "no answer" is not included.

particular difficulties for women, either because of their low numbers or their balancing act between career and family. For example, time management/balancing committee responsibilities with research and teaching (response 2) can be a problem for both male and female faculty. However, because of their low numbers in science and engineering, women faculty are often asked to serve on more committees to meet gender diversity needs, even while they are still junior, and to advise more students, either formally or informally (NSF, 1997). Cutthroat competition makes it difficult for both men and women to succeed and obtain funding. Gender stereotypes that reinforce women's socialization to be less overtly competitive may make it more difficult for a woman scientist or engineer to succeed in a very competitive environment. Category D (responses 9, 11, 13, and 14) identifies barriers of overt harassment and discrimination faced by women scientists and engineers. Sometimes even a positive response, such as active recruitment of women/more opportunities (response 10), leads to backlash and difficulties in gaining credibility from peers who assume the woman obtained the position because of affirmative action.

By looking more closely at some of the quotations from the respondents from all 4 years, we can learn the qualitative context for the categories and gain greater insight into the problems at hand. The women express the specific barriers for their careers.

*Category A. Pressures women face in balancing career and family*

> For me the difficulty is balancing a "normal" family life with a "successful" career in science. I know that if I spent more hours on work-related activities (like writing manuscripts, improving my lecture, writing proposals) that I would be more productive. Instead, I choose to work a normal work week of ca. 40 hours a week, and when I am at home, I am totally at home ... doing little else other than playing with my children, cleaning house and spending quality time with my husband. I know that I probably will never be as "successful" as the person who devotes 60–80 hours per week working, and sometimes it is frustrating, but it's a choice that I have made. (1999 respondent 12)
>
> As a person who relocated her job from Korea to U.S., I do not feel apparent discrimination here when hiring woman scientists.

However, the most significant issues/challenges for woman scientists are how to combine the work with family when they are married. Oftentimes, they are the ones who face difficulties to pursue their careers fully since it is not always feasible to find/relocate jobs in the area where their husbands' jobs are located. In the case of relocation, one could lose the establishment built up in the previous position. The situation gets worse when they have children under kindergarten age. Unlike other fields, it is not plausible for a woman scientist, especially for those doing "hard" science, to work part-time or resume her career after a break, for instance, if she stays home for a few years to take care of her child[ren]. (1999 respondent 24)

Managing dual career families (particularly dual academic careers). Often women take the lesser position in such a situation. Ph.D. women are often married to Ph.D. men. Most Ph.D. men are not married to Ph.D. women. (2000 respondent 16)

For me, the biggest issue was children — not just the physical act of bearing them. But the emotional act each day of raising them. I'm unusual for a female researcher. I had two children in graduate school and still finished in 4 years. Now I'm trudging along trying to get tenure, having become a single mother along the way — no one's stopped my clock or bought me out of a course. No institution has ever given me a break. While I've had a couple of wonderful fairy godfathers in my career (which is probably why I'm still in this career at all), the institutions themselves have felt quite cold and unforgiving. I *know* that a huge amount of my creative energy is siphoned away from my research into their lives and development. I *know* that if I were a male with a wife at home raising the children, my work would be different. But the institutions have no way of dealing with this inequity. (1998 respondent 11)

Although balancing career and family stands out as the overwhelming difficulty faced by women scientists and engineers, as the quotations document, the particular form of that problem varies depending upon factors such as life stage, marital status, and career of spouse or partner.

*Category B. Problems women face because of their low numbers and stereotypes held by others regarding gender*

Low numbers lead to increased visibility for those in the minority. Such visibility can have both positive and negative consequences. Negative consequences include assumptions by others that the individual represents and exhibits behavior and ideas held by all other women (stereotyping). An individual who does well stands out and often experiences positives consequences, such as fast career tracks and opportunities, because the male majority remember her outstanding, anomalous performance.

Although possibly less now than before, women scientists still comprise a small proportion of professors in tenure-track positions. Thus, there are few "models" to emulate and few to get advice/mentoring from. Although men could also mentor, there are unique experiences for women that perhaps can only be felt and shared by other women faculty, particularly in other Ph.D. granting institutions. Some examples of this: a different (i.e., more challenging) treatment by undergraduate and graduate students of women faculty than they would of male faculty; difficulties in dealing with agencies outside of the university who are used to dealing with male professors; difficulties related to managing demands of scholarship and grantsmanship with maternity demands. More women in a department would possibly allow a better environment for new women faculty members to thrive in such a department through advice/mentoring and more awareness of issues facing women faculty members. (2000 respondent 26)

There remains a disconnect between women faculty and the upper administration of universities, which is male dominated. The natural tendency to pass on information in casual networks can lead to exclusion of women from the inner circles of information, not necessarily maliciously, but just due to human nature. (2000 respondent 51)

The biggest challenge that women face in planning a career in science is not being taken seriously. Often women have to go farther, work harder and accomplish more in order to be recognized. (2000 respondent 21)

Opportunities are there. Applications from women are less likely to be cast aside without careful examination in any field where they are under-represented. That is, the first step in affirmative action works. Yet old biases can creep back in during the scrutiny that follows. Opportunities can be limited by failure of male leaders to mentor women as effectively as they might their young male protégés. (1999 respondent 43)

I think women have to prove their competence; whereas men have to prove their incompetence. For example, I have often heard men question whether a particular woman scientist (say, one who is defending her thesis or is interviewing for a faculty position) actually contributed substantially to the work she presents; whereas, I have never heard a man questioned on this. (1997 respondent 6)

*Category C. Issues faced by both men and women scientists and engineers in the current environment of tight resources, which may pose particular difficulties for women.*

Also, the fact that there are fewer women than men on most campuses also puts women in the position of having to do a disproportionate amount of committee service, as many committees attempt to have representation by women faculty. (1999 respondent 83)

I still find the strong perception that women should be doing more teaching and service because of the expectation that women are more nurturing. Although research as a priority for women is given a lot of lip service, I've not seen a lot of support for it. (2000 respondent 1)

*Category D. More overt discrimination and/or harassment.*

I am now 25 years post-Ph.D. and have worked in a number of institutional settings — in several of them I was the only woman or one of two or three. I think the social environments are improving — primarily due to federal civil rights laws. I do believe, however, that women are still strongly differently treated and are often subjected to unnecessary or excessive social aggression or are just plain blocked out of resource access. Most of this is subtle but damaging. (1999 respondent 59)

I have often buffered the bad behavior of my colleagues — and over the years I have handled a number of sexual harassment or "hostile supervision" cases where a more senior person (all of them male) was behaving inappropriately toward a lower social status woman (or in rarer cases a gay man). (1999 respondent 59)

In general, the academic community is fairly "enlightened" when it comes to gender equality in undergraduate education. However, as you move up the ladder into masters and doctoral programs, you start to see increasing amounts of "sexism." Thus, it is my opinion that the most significant challenge to women scientists is to develop a set of "people skills" that allow them to obtain/achieve technical opportunities and promotions within the male-dominated system. The glass ceiling is all too real, thus I think women must not only achieve technically as men do, but figure out how to make the system work for them, which is different from the "entitlement" mode of career paths for men. (1997 respondent 71)

Although family responsibilities become difficult to balance with work for some men who take on significant child care responsibilities, balancing the tenure clock with the biological clock challenges women scientists and engineers who want to become biological mothers in ways never faced by men since they cannot become pregnant. The two-career problem provides difficulties for both men and women. Most (62%) female scientists and engineers are also married to male scientists and engineers, who are also often in the same field. The reverse is not the case because the majority of scientists are men and are married to women who are not scientists or engineers (Sonnert & Holton, 1995).

Continuing low numbers of women in many science, engineering, and mathematics fields provides other particular challenges and some opportunities. Low numbers means that women often serve as the first or one of few women in their department and college. Women may have no senior women colleagues, may be asked to serve on more committees (even at the junior level), and are asked to advise (either formally or informally) more students (NSF, 1997).

Although these service activities may not be valued by the institution for promotion and tenure and may lead to difficulties with time management, they also provide opportunities for women to be visible and to experience leadership and administration at an early stage in their careers. Similarly, the low numbers that result in active recruitment of women into many areas of science, engineering, and mathematics have both positive and negative consequences. Demand in engineering and computer science gives women starting salaries that are equal to or higher than those of their male counterparts (Vetter, 1996). The recruitment can lead to various forms of backlash for a woman, ranging from overt discrimination to difficulties gaining credibility from peers and administrators who assume she obtained the position to fill a quota. Ironically, POWRE, because it is an award for women that attempts to address some of these issues, is often perceived as less credible and prestigious by male scientists and administrators, despite its 20% success rate, which makes it more competitive than most NSF grants.

As with most experiences, the general statistical trends emerge from particular situations that occur on a frequent schedule and become mitigated or exacerbated by individual laboratory climates and disciplinary cultures. The average routine for women in the laboratory environment, as explored in Chapter 3, provides insights into positive and negative climates that enhance or inhibit research productivity and quality of life for women scientists and engineers.

# CHAPTER 3
## LIFE IN THE LAB

The laboratory climate makes a tremendous difference. Everyone needs a work environment that is comfortable, supportive, and non-threatening. I feel fortunate to have this now, at this stage in my career, but I know that many women do not. My sense is that younger women are often not taken seriously enough in their work environment and many women are excluded from important informal information exchange that goes on in the laboratory. I have had to work extra hard to build and maintain good communication with my colleagues here. (1997 respondent 24)

Although everyone agrees that an appropriate, supportive work environment usually aids in building a successful career, neither the nature of the laboratory climate in general nor gender differences in the climate and their impacts on women's careers in particular have been studied thoroughly. A few observational studies by sociologists of science have examined laboratory climate. Sharon Traweek (1988) describes high-energy physics laboratories in *Beamtimes and Lifetimes*. Bruno Latour and Steven Woolgar (1979) revealed laboratory practices in immunology, and Bruno Latour (1987) explored technology. Although these studies have tended to mention gender issues in passing, if at all, Traweek describes the laboratory as a man's world from which women have been marginalized:

> In the fifteen years I have been visiting physics labs, the status of women within them has remained unchanged — in spite of major transformations, in North America and Europe, in opportunities for women and attitudes about their roles. In this book, women remain marginal, as they are in the laboratory. The lab is a man's world, and I try to show how that is particularly the case in high-energy physics: how the practice of physics is engendered, how laboratory work is masculinized. (1988, p. 16).

The study by Judith McIlwee and Gregg Robinson (1992) explored the culture of the laboratory in engineering for women:

> [There's] a lot of competition. A lot of competition. These are very intelligent bright people we're talking about. CDI's a high tech company, and they hire the top ten percent. There's an awful lot of competition. You need to be confident about what you do, and from my own personal point of view, that was a hard thing to find. (p. 117)

A growing body of literature focuses on female-friendly teaching techniques, including teaching in the laboratory, such as group work, women-only classes, and guided-design problems, that have been demonstrated to be particularly effective for attracting and retaining women and girls (Barad, 1995; Richardson, Sutton, & Cercone, 1995; Rosser, 1990, 1995, 1997). Contributing to the interest in science, engineering, mathematics, and technology curricular and teaching reform at the K–12 (AAAS, 1990; 1993; AAUW, 1992; NRC, 1996) and undergraduate levels (Tobias, 1990, 1992; Project Kaleidoscope, 1994), this work does little to address the laboratory climate for women at the graduate, postdoctoral, or professional level. Because the ratio of women to men decreases at each increasing level of the hierarchy, studies of factors that contribute to the dropout rate at the higher levels would be useful. The study by McIlwee and Robinson (1992) again sheds some light on the situation for women engineers:

Let us return to our earlier question regarding Ginger's reasons for taking a "demotion" out of the lab. Ginger's initial account of her decision was that she did not like that kind of engineering. She was more people-oriented, and felt estranged by the single-minded technical orientation of the lab. When we pursued this issue with her, however, it became more complex. Ginger found it difficult to put her finger on just exactly what it was that drove her out. If she had enjoyed the technical work more, she would have stayed. But she would have enjoyed it more if she had not felt so isolated and unappreciated. She knew that upper-level management looked kindly on her and was encouraging her to pursue graduate work, but the engineers in the lab seemed unappreciative and distant. She had no mentor, nor even any encouragement from those around her. (p. 124)

Question 2: How does the laboratory climate (or its equivalent in your subdiscipline) impact upon the careers of women scientists?

The second question on the e-mail quesitonnaire attempted to explore women's perceptions of their daily work environment. Studies of work climates have shown that employee perceptions of the same environment vary greatly. Two scientists sharing the same office or laboratory may have entirely different perceptions. Race, gender, status, and other factors may lead to differences in perception. Conversely, a given environment may not operate uniformly, neutrally, or androgynously because of such factors (Fox, 1985).

Some studies (Britton, 1997; Wright & Saylor, 1992) suggest that women like their workplace when they have effective supervisors, and men like it when they have other colleagues "like themselves." Fox (1991) finds that the same institutional setting (major university, minor university, or liberal arts college) may offer different constraints and opportunities for one gender compared to the other. She states, "Within the same type of setting, women scientists can have fewer and different collaborative arrangements, claims to enabling administrative favors, collegial opportunities for testing and developing ideas, and entrees into the informal culture of science and scholarship" (p. 204). Even within the same occupational setting (BA or Ph.D.-granting department, tenure status) gender groups may have different opportunities, resources, and privileges. For example, the nature and quality of collegial interaction may differ for women who speak with faculty members once a term rather than once a week, as do their male colleagues (Fox, 1991). Richard and Krieshok (1989) observe that rank and stress may operate differently in men and women: "Whereas strain decreased for males as they moved up in rank it tended to increase for females as they were promoted" (p. 128). These studies suggest that perceptions of the same workplace climate do vary among individuals and that gender is one of many factors that may interact with that perception.

Question 2 of the e-mail survey attempted to explore women's perceptions of their work environment. As with question 1, data from question 2 are not conducive to standard tests of means for award years and directorates. While we cannot conclude statistical differences between years or directorates, notable trends do emerge when the frequencies of responses are analyzed by award year and directorate. In fiscal years 1997, 1998, and 1999, balancing career and family/time away from home (the same response as for question 1) was an answer given by more respondents than any other. As Table 8 documents, in contrast to question 1, the responses given to this question reflect less consensus. Awardees from all years, but particularly 1997 awardees, had some difficulty understanding the question. Although many women did not mention problems in either their laboratory or work environment related to gender issues (responses 3, 4, and 9), the largest number of responses did suggest that to some degree their gender led to their being perceived as a problem, anomaly, or deviant from the norm in the laboratory/work environment. Awardees for 1998 and 1999 ranked hostile or intimidating environment (response 7) higher than 1997 and 2000 awardees. Awardees for 1999 ranked the boys' club atmosphere (response 6), lack of numbers/networking (response 11), and lack of funding (response 16) as more problematic than did 1997, 1998, or 2000 awardees. In contrast, 1998 awardees ranked have not experienced problems (response 3) and positive impact (response 10) higher than either 1997 or 1999 awardees. The 2000 awardees ranked positive impact (response 10) and lack of camaraderie/communications and isolation (response 5) higher than any of the previous 3 years of awardees. Awardees for 1999 and 2000 also mentioned new issues not articulated by 1997 or 1998 awardees, such as space (response 21), cultural/national stereotypes for women (response 20), and department doesn't get basic issues (response 19).

### Categorization of Responses

A phase model that was originally developed to examine stages of integration of information on women into the curriculum (McIntosh, 1984; Schuster & Van Dyne, 1995) has proven useful in looking at science, mathematics, engineering, and technology curriculum and pedagogy (Rosser, 1990, 1995). I thought this model might also be used to categorize and examine effects of perceived laboratory climate on careers of women scientists. Socialization (Davis et al., 1996), organization (Fox, 1995, 1996; Sonnert & Holton, 1995) and other structural factors (Allaire & Firsirotu, 1984) may impact women's entrance and retention in science, engineering, and mathematics. The widely varying percentages of women in the different science and engineering disciplines suggest that disciplinary culture also impacts women's retention or entrance into the field, as discussed in Chapter 4. Because the NSF divides its directorates by discipline and awards POWRE grants through each directorate, the disciplinary or directorate affiliation constituted a primary piece of datum known about each awardee. A framework focused on disciplinary and laboratory culture thus provided a useful tool to analyze the responses.

I applied a five-stage version of the phase model to assess the extent to which women have been integrated fully into the laboratory and its climate has been adapted to include/incorporate women's needs and contributions. Colleagues in the same laboratory as awardees were not queried, and many awardees have no female colleagues. Although the categorization I implemented was far from objective and independent, the phase model provides a beginning step in grouping responses.

> Stage 1: Absence of women not noted. This is the traditional laboratory consisting of men. Originally populated by White, middle-to upper-class European and North American men, the laboratory climate reflects their values, approaches, and lifestyles. Absence of women is not noted; it is assumed that gender affects neither who becomes a scientist nor the science produced.

**TABLE 8** Total Responses to Question 2

Question 2: How does the laboratory climate (or its equivalent in your subdiscipline) impact upon the careers of women scientists?

| | CATEGORIES | 1997 % OF RESPONSES | | 1998 % OF RESPONSES | | 1999 % OF RESPONSES | | 2000 % OF RESPONSES | |
|---|---|---|---|---|---|---|---|---|---|
| 1 | Don't know/question unclear | 16.4 | (11/67) | 4.2 | (5/119) | 7.1 | (7/98) | 5.7 | (6/105) |
| 2 | Balancing career and family/time away from home | 13.4 | (9/67) | 19.3 | (23/119) | 16.3 | (16/98) | 13.3 | (14/105) |
| 3 | Have not experienced problems | 11.9 | (8/67) | 16.8 | (20/119) | 10.2 | (10/98) | 9.5 | (10/105) |
| 4 | Not in lab atmosphere/can't answer | 11.9 | (8/67) | 5.9 | (7/119) | 1.0 | (1/98) | 8.6 | (9/105) |
| 5 | Lack of camaraderie/communications and isolation | 9.0 | (6/67) | 11.8 | (14/119) | 9.2 | (9/98) | 14.3 | (15/105) |
| 6 | "Boy's club" atmosphere | 9.0 | (6/67) | 9.2 | (11/119) | 18.4 | (18/98) | 9.5 | (10/105) |
| 7 | Hostile environment/intimidating/lack of authority | 9.0 | (6/67) | 14.3 | (17/119) | 15.3 | (15/98) | 8.6 | (9/105) |
| 8 | Establishing respectability/credibility | 9.0 | (6/67) | 10.9 | (13/119) | 10.2 | (10/98) | 3.8 | (4/105) |
| 9 | No answer | 7.5 | (5/67) | 6.7 | (8/119) | 5.1 | (5/98) | <1 | (1/105) |
| 10 | Positive impact | 6.0 | (4/67) | 10.1 | (12/119) | 6.1 | (6/98) | 11.4 | (12/105) |
| 11 | Lack of numbering/networking | 4.5 | (3/67) | 6.7 | (8/119) | 12.2 | (12/98) | 4.8 | (5/105) |
| 12 | General problem with time management | 4.5 | (3/67) | 1.7 | (2/119) | 5.1 | (5/98) | 3.8 | (4/105) |
| 13 | Safety concerns/presence of toxic substances (health concerns) | 3.0 | (2/67) | 0 | (0/119) | 4.1 | (4/98) | 1.9 | (2/105) |
| 14 | Benefit by working with peers | 3.0 | (2/67) | 2.5 | (3/119) | 3.1 | (3/98) | 5.7 | (6/105) |
| 15 | Problem of wanting research independence | 3.0 | (2/67) | 0 | (0/119) | 1.0 | (1/98) | <1 | (1/105) |
| 16 | Lack of funding | 1.5 | (1/67) | <1 | (1/119) | 5.1 | (5/98) | <1 | (1/105) |
| 17 | Benefit from time flexibility/determine own lab hours | 3.0 | (2/67) | 1.7 | (2/119) | 3.1 | (3/98) | 1.9 | (2/105) |
| 18 | Did not answer | 0 | (0/67) | 0 | (0/119) | 3.1 | (3/98) | 0 | (0/105) |
| 19 | Department doesn't understand basic issues | -- | | -- | | -- | | <1 | (1/105) |
| 20 | Cultural/national stereotypes for women | -- | | -- | | -- | | 6.7 | (7/105) |
| 21 | Space | -- | | -- | | 1.0 | (1/98) | 0 | (0/105) |
| 22 | Better bathroom facilities | -- | | -- | | -- | | <1 | (1/105) |

Stage 2: Women as an add-on. At this stage, some women have entered the traditional laboratory. The women have had little or no impact upon the laboratory climate or the men in the laboratory, although each action undertaken by a woman scientist or engineer may become especially salient or completely ignored because of her gender. The women are tolerated/accepted in the laboratory, as long as they assume (or at least do not challenge by their own behavior in terms of hours worked, interaction styles, socialization patterns, problems studied) the male-as-norm value, approaches, and lifestyles.

Stage 3: Women as a problem, anomaly, or deviant from the norm. At this stage, women challenge the male-as-norm laboratory climate. The challenge may come from a variety of angles — request for maternity leave; working shorter hours because of children, relationship, or other interests; search for more collaborative, less confrontational interaction styles with colleagues; desire for mentoring by senior faculty.

Stage 4: Focus on women. At this stage, both the women and the men in the laboratory begin to consider and focus on positive benefits that might accrue from a change in laboratory climate or from having a diversity of styles (some of which might be correlated with gender) in the laboratory.

Stage 5: A laboratory climate redefined and reconsidered to include us all.

This represents the ideal laboratory environment where all feel included and the diversity promotes creativity.

The division of the responses into one of the five stages remains quite subjective and dependent upon the interpretation of what the scientist meant when she used certain words. Some responses might have been placed in more than one stage; others reflected aspects of more than one stage.

*Stage 1: Absence of women not noted.*
I placed don't know/question unclear (response 1), have not experienced problems (response 3), not in lab atmosphere/can't answer (response 4), and no answer (response 9) in stage 1. At this phase,

scientists and engineers fail to notice, or actively ignore, any gender issues arising in the laboratory. They reflect the notion that gender affects neither who becomes a scientist nor the kind of science produced. The following answer reflects an answer categorized as stage 1:

> Not sure I understand what you want to know here. If you don't like research, then the laboratory climate would deter you from a career in science. I like research so it wasn't a problem. (1997 respondent 29)

In this stage, I also included responses that said "I don't understand the question" (response 1) because this response implied possible lack of understanding of how cultural norms surrounding gender and gender dynamics from the broader society might be replicated in laboratory hierarchies, communications, and access to equipment and resources. An alternative interpretation might be that respondents did not know what the jargon "laboratory climate" means, which might or might not indicate a lack of awareness of gender issues.

### Stage 2: Women as add-on.

I placed general problems with time management (response 12), safety concerns/presence of toxic substances (response 13), lack of funding (response 16), space (response 21), and better bathroom facilities (response 22) in this stage. Although leaving the door open to the possibility of a gender component of laboratory environment, this stage assumes everyone faces essentially the same condition and that women should change or accommodate to the laboratory environment to maintain the status quo of the male style in the laboratory. The following responses exemplify this stage.

> In my field we don't have laboratories, but we do have clics (*sic*) and groups of researchers that are usually led by male researchers — although there are some good female researchers in my field. I think the bottom line is that you have to be good, and so good (if you're male or female) that people want to work with you. (1997 respondent 34)
>
> There is little recognition of the contradiction that researchers are expected to spend personal time in the lab doing research, when espe-

cially women are expected to spend their personal time for family obligations. (2000 respondent 1)

*Stage 3: Women as a problem, anomaly, or deviation from the norm.*
This became the stage into which I placed the most responses—balancing career and family/time away from home (response 2), lack of camaraderie/communications and isolation (response 5), "boys' club" atmosphere (response 6), hostile environment/intimidating/lack of authority (response 7), establishing respectability/credibility (response 8), problem of wanting research independence (response 15), department doesn't understand basic issues (response 19), and cultural/ national stereotypes for women (response 20). Although varying by discipline and subfield, most women perceived some problems or difficulties of the laboratory climate that impacted their careers.

The following comments illustrate the range of the problems from reluctance to cast women in the role of leaders in the laboratory through questions about field competence, to discrimination by men from foreign countries that hold a very traditional view of women's roles.

> In the laboratory situations, women are often considered followers rather than leaders; consequently, it is difficult for women to assume leading roles. (1997 respondent 23)
>
> Science does tend to require long hours. If I had a young family, I'm sure these long hours would be hard to maintain, setting me back in terms of a career, especially with the rapidly approaching tenure decision. In my field, I also spend a great deal of time doing research at sea (two or three months every year). A supportive spouse is a key requirement for keeping this up. My problem is that my fieldwork is in the summer, which is also the only time away from teaching that I could spend near my spouse. It used to be harder for a woman just to get on the ship to do her work, but now that women are allowed on most ships (not all, nuclear submarines are apparently still off-limits), this aspect of our science is less of a problem than it used to be. Progress! (1997 respondent 22)
>
> The laboratory climate in my field negatively impacts the careers of women scientists. Many of my colleagues are foreign males who do

not take females seriously and do not collaborate with them. (2000 respondent 62)

Personally I have been able to work in the lab environment without difficulty. However, I have found that my female students seem to know less practical laboratory skills, and are frequently kidded or even harassed about it. I have seen this lead to becoming more withdrawn and a feeling of alienation and self-doubt, and they never get a chance to improve their practical laboratory skills. Frequently, it seems that only the very strong or the very determined feel that they have a place in the laboratory. (1997 respondent 19)

In my field I think women face greater challenges in relation to their fieldwork. My colleagues and I have all worked in the field — conducting behavioral, ecological, and physiological research. But I think there is still a level of discrimination against women — can she really do fieldwork as well as a man? I think women face some real challenges related to personal safety when they are in the field, especially when they are alone. This affects the ability of women to function exactly like a man, but it does not prevent women from doing excellent field research, but working in teams or at field stations or working alone if they are willing to do so. (1998 respondent 12)

Computer science laboratories appear to be especially problematic for women at both the professional and pre-professional levels.

Computer labs in high schools and universities are frequently dominated by macho cliques or "computer jocks." Their culture and behavior tend to intimidate and/or turn off most female students, and even some male students. (1997 respondent 7)

The lab environment does intimidate the women in computer science. There are a lot of male hackers who know the in's and out's of how to use a computer and they can be very condescending to people who lack the background, but have the same or more ability to succeed. There are too many egos that drive this attitude, rather than cooperative attitudes. I hear this concern from women just beginning grad school or undergrad computer science, regularly. (1998 respondent 85)

*Stage 4: Focus on women.*

Positive impact (response 10), benefit by working with peers (response 14), and benefit from time flexibility/determine own lab hours (response 17) might be classified as stage 4. This stage suggests the particular and positive approaches women might bring to the laboratory environment to be fostered and ways in which the laboratory environment facilitates women's work and lives. The emphasis at this stage moves from women fitting in (stage 2) to what new insights, openness, and approaches might emerge from having diverse people coming from different experiences working on a problem.

> I think it impacts in two different ways. Women tend to nurture in their labs. They are reluctant to fire the people they should fire and they tend to do more hand holding and sympathizing than whip cracking. So in some ways they can fall into the trap of being a mom to the lab members rather than a boss. I also think that the current climate requires that you be in the lab 10 hours a day six days a week. This is hard on everyone but especially on those with a family. (1997 respondent 35)

Some respondents suggest that the subculture (or perhaps the critical mass of women) permits more or less flexibility for women to demonstrate their creativity.

> I think it may be a bit easier in the social sciences, which do not have the traditional hierarchical laboratory structure as in the natural sciences. There is a bit more freedom to structure one's lab in a variety of ways. (1997 respondent 18)
>
> In many fields of chemistry, the laboratory climate is detrimental to the careers of women scientists. Indeed, many women leave the field of organic chemistry primarily because of the climate. Alternatively, the numbers of women in physical and analytical chemistry (my areas), continue to grow. (1998 respondent 30)

*Stage 5: A laboratory climate redefined and reconsidered to include us all.*

None of the response categories themselves fit stage 5, the phase for which we strive, because this stage would allow the most creative, productive work from all scientists, regardless of their gender, to make a better science. Attracting and retaining a critical mass of women in each subdiscipline in science, engineering, mathematics, and technology provide the first steps toward creating a favorable laboratory climate. Acceptance of diverse approaches, lifestyles, and alternatives to problem-solving creates supportive work environments in which all scientists are likely to thrive.

Because many women have life experiences that differ from those of their male colleagues, these experiences may lead women scientists and engineers to different approaches, interests, and questions to their research from those traditionally used by men (Keller, 1983; Rosser, 1990, 1997). As in identifying the difficulties, the words of the respondents themselves, provide the most convincing evidence for the potential of new ideas and approaches women can contribute to science and engineering.

> The best opportunities I have seen are the chances to work in areas which have been neglected because they fall somewhere between traditional disciplinary boundaries. Ease of communication (particularly e-mail and the web) means that it is easier to contact and collaborate with people outside one's own immediate field of research. It has been said that women scientists tend to collaborate more than men; if this is true, then these opportunities may be greater for women. Ease of communication can also make women feel less isolated even when they work in male-dominated fields. (1999 respondent 44)
>
> The emphasis of my research is centered on computers because of my physical limitations. In this area I think women can excel. In my experience I find that certain elements in a woman's temperament (e.g., diligence in pursuing the source of a problem) make women more proficient in solving computer problems. In addition, the flexibility of scheduling work on a personal computer should benefit women who must juggle the responsibilities of home and a career. (1997 respondent 82)

Suggestions implied by the quotations exemplifying stage 5 move the issue beyond the level of numbers and equity to positive benefits of diversity for improving science and engineering. Because women have different experiences and socialization, they may approach problems differently, work together in collaborative groups more easily, and attend to particular or different details than their male colleagues. These different approaches, interests, and ways of working hold the potential to benefit science and engineering, which thrive on new perspectives and diverse ways of looking at the world.

# CHAPTER 4
## DIFFERENCES ACROSS THE DISCIPLINES

### Computer Engineer Rose Sumat

Rose started in computer engineering as a freshman at the large, prestigious Midwestern public institution and really never waivered from her decision, going on to receive her BS and MS in the field at the same institution. Although not many women pursued degrees in engineering, especially electrical engineering, she learned to look for the one or two women in each class and hang out with them. The professors were supportive, but occasionally the male students would make negative suggestions such as, "You got that internship because you're a girl." Her father, who was an electrical engineer and an academic, clearly served as a role model and influence toward her choice of a major. At the time, she had some idea that she wanted a Ph.D., but she thought she needed some experience in industry.

After 5 years in the East at a major computer firm, Rose was ready for graduate school. She moved to the West to a large, public institution. She realized that she had missed academia and its particular approaches to problem solving; industry seemed less challenging and more repetitious.

When Rose received her Ph.D., she decided to stay in academia. Fortunately, her decision coincided with an improvement in the academic job market. She obtained a tenure-track position at a prestigious Northeastern private institution. Although the discipline of electrical engineering continues to be overwhelmingly male, she learned to adapt. Rose recognized that women were welcome, as long as they conform to the male image and expectations for the field.

Receiving a POWRE award really helped Rose to get her research under way, providing seed money to pursue a new project for which she didn't yet have results. Almost simultaneously she received a NSF CAREER award. Despite these two prestigious awards, getting started was difficult. Being the only person doing systems computer engineering at her relatively small school of engineering meant that obtaining graduate students was not easy; at one point, she had money and no students to support. Eventually, the money helped to attract students. She actually extended the POWRE award for a longer period because she had two maternity leaves in relatively short succession. When she applied for subsequent NSF funding, she stated that POWRE had allowed her to start this new direction in her work.

Juggling her academic career with two small children provides a constant struggle. Although Rose used her institution's relatively liberal policies, including a stoppage of the tenure clock and the option of not teaching during the semester following childbirth, starting a career and a family at the same time is difficult. For example, not teaching after the birth of her child retarded the formation of her research group because she couldn't teach a graduate course to facilitate attracting graduate students to her research group; conversely, not teaching was absolutely necessary for her family and other parts of her research. Rose's story underlines the difficulties in balancing career and family as the major issue for women in science and engineering.

As documented in the introductory chapter, the percentage of women has increased during the past 3 decades in varying amounts in all disciplines except computer science. Table 1 includes the data given in the introductory chapter for the percentage of women receiving BS, MS, and Ph.D. degrees in the different disciplines of science and engineering. Table 2 shows the NSF data for different faculty ranks in different science and engineering disciplines; Table 3 documents the percentage of women compared to men who hold tenure at different types of institutions. As with most data sets, these data reveal more than one trend or significant point.

Vertical segregation — decreasing percentages of women scientists compared to their male counterparts with increasing levels of hierarchy (BS to MS to Ph.D. to faculty, and with higher faculty ranks) — emerges from comparisons of Tables 1, 2, and 3. The metaphor of the "leaky pipeline" has often been used to describe this vertical segregation where women are lost at every stage from high school to faculty. Some studies (Kulis, Sciotte, & Collins, , 2002; Valian, 1998) have focused particularly on the factors that lead to women's attrition and slower promotion to the higher ranks of academia. Chapters 1, 2, and 3 have centered on quantitative and qualitative examples that describe and explain some of the parameters leading to this vertical segregation.

Table 7 also reveals horizontal segregation — differential gender segregation by disciplines within science and engineering. Psychology, where women earn the overwhelming majority of degrees at all levels, represents one extreme, sometimes characterized as the "feminized" discipline, while engineering, where women earn less than 20% of degrees at all levels, represents the other "masculinized" extreme. Within each of these broader disciplines, the various subdisciplines also exhibit horizontal segregation with regard to gender (Valian, 1998). For example, in 1996, women earned 32% of the bachelor's degrees in civil engineering, but only 12% of the degrees in mechanical engineering. Within the social sciences, in 1996 women earned 73% of the undergraduate degrees in psychology, but only 30% of the degrees in economics (NSF, 2000, Table 2–7).

As the responses of the women to the question about laboratory climate discussed in Chapter 3 reveal, disciplines and subfields of research have their own particularities and cultures. Spending time in the field or weeks on a ship creates a different environment and culture than the laboratory environment. Working with a team of collaborators differs substantially from isolated work with cell cultures or hours alone on the computer.

Substantial differences that characterize the cultures of the different disciplines in science, engineering, mathematics, and technology contribute to notions of climate in each field. These characteristics are often viewed as particularly attractive to one gender. The very competitive, hierarchical, and equipment-intensive climate often associated with the physics laboratory has been cited (Keller, 1985; Latour, 1987) as a male-dominated environment less likely to attract women. Working in isolation, involved with hardware, and obsession with hacking may describe computer scientists in their laboratories (Bohonak, 1995; Eastman, 1995). In contrast, some areas of the social sciences, such as areas of cultural anthropology, may be viewed as people-oriented and egalitarian because of their methods of ethnography and participant observation. These more collaborative methods and interactions with people are seen as female friendly (Rosser, 1990). Much of engineering uses teams, emphasizing large group projects. In many areas such as theoretical mathematics, political science, or economics, the terms "laboratory environment" may not be directly applicable.

In addition to differences in disciplinary and subdisciplinary cultures within science, engineering, mathematics, and technology, large discrepancies in the actual percentages of women in the different disciplines and subdisciplines further complicate the issues (Kulis et al., 2002; Valian, 1998). The connection between subdisciplinary characteristics regarding laboratory climate and percentages of women appears difficult to sever. Are women deterred from a field such as physics because it is perceived as competitive, hierarchical, and equipment intensive? Or does the overwhelming predominance of men create a laboratory environment (and approach to science) emphasizing these characteristics, which, because they are linked with masculinity in our culture (Keller, 1985; Traweek, 1988), tend to deter women from the field? Because of such differences in disciplinary culture and vertical gender segregation, I disaggregated the responses of the women to questions 1 and 2 to explore disciplinary differences.

Table 9 shows the responses to question 1 when the data from all 4 years are pooled and the responses are categorized by the NSF directorate of the awardee; this categorization assumes that the NSF directorate granting the POWRE award serves as an indicator of the discipline or field of the awardee. (Note that for data interpretation, education and human resources [EHR] is removed since the numbers are smaller and all awardees come from disciplinary backgrounds included in other NSF directorates.) Perhaps the most striking finding is the overall similarity among the directorates. Balancing work with family responsibilities (response 1) stands out overwhelmingly as the major issue for women from all directorates, just as it did for awardees for all years.

The top six responses were fairly consistent across all directorates, with few exceptions. For mathematics and physical sciences (MPS), low numbers of women, isolation, and lack of camaraderie/mentoring (response 3) was lower and positive; active recruitment of women/more opportunities (response 10) was higher than for other directorates. This response is curious, given that MPS includes physics, where low numbers of women have been a problem. However, MPS also includes chemistry and mathematics, fields where women have increased substantially and where job opportunities are plentiful; this may account for the positive response. Both engineering (ENG) and geosciences (GEO) gave relatively high response rates to response 10. Again, this may reflect the positive job opportunities in these fields at the time of the survey, although both of these directorates gave a high response to affirmative action/backlash/discrimination (response 9). Computer and information science and engineering (CISE) and biology (BIO) awardees also gave a higher response to response 9, although a less strong response to 10. Note that when the 16 responses are grouped into the four categories of Table 10, some of the nuances are lost. For example, category B includes both responses 3 and 10, which as noted above are respectively lower and higher for MPS in Table 9. MPS appears similar to other directorates when responses 3 and 10 are grouped together in category B in Table 10.

Quotations from the responses of the women themselves best elucidate some of disciplinary differences:

> I am an organic chemist, and this area has been heavily dominated by men. In labs that I have been in as a postdoctoral fellow, many women graduate students (and myself, come to think of it ) were sexually harassed in minor or major ways. Many female graduate students dropped out in these high pressure, male dominated labs. (1998 respondent 21)

**TABLE 9** Responses to Question 1 According to Directorate

Question 1: What are the most significant issues/challenges/opportunities facing women scientists today as they plan their careers?

| CATEGORIES | SBE % OF RESPONSES | MPS % OF RESPONSES | ENG % OF RESPONSES | EHR[a] % OF RESPONSES | CISE % OF RESPONSES | BIO % OF RESPONSES | GEO % OF RESPONSES |
|---|---|---|---|---|---|---|---|
| 1 Balancing work with family responsibilities (children, elderly relatives, etc.) | 60.3 (38/63) | 77.4 (65/84) | 65.2 (45/69) | 91.7 (11/12) | 60.0 (21/35) | 82.4 (70/85) | 73.7 (28/38) |
| 2 Time management/balancing committee responsibilities with research and teaching | 15.7 (10/63) | 13.1 (11/84) | 11.6 (8/69) | 0 (0/12) | 17.1 (6/35) | 12.9 (11/85) | 21.1 (8/38) |
| 3 Low numbers of women, isolation and lack of camaraderie/mentoring | 23.8 (15/63) | 11.9 (10/84) | 21.7 (15/69) | 33.3 (4/12) | 31.4 (11/35) | 20.0 (17/85) | 39.5 (15/38) |
| 4 Gaining credibility/respectability from peers and administrators | 17.5 (11/63) | 20.2 (17/84) | 24.6 (17/69) | 25.0 (3/12) | 31.4 (11/35) | 16.5 (14/85) | 13.2 (5/38) |
| 5 "Two career" problem (balance with spouse's career) | 14.3 (9/63) | 28.6 (24/84) | 13.0 (9/69) | 16.7 (2/12) | 22.9 (8/35) | 11.8 (10/85) | 21.1 (8/38) |
| 6 Lack of funding/inability to get funding | 4.8 (3/63) | 7.1 (6/84) | 8.7 (6/69) | 0 (0/12) | 5.7 (2/35) | 8.2 (7/85) | 10.5 (4/38) |
| 7 Job restrictions (location, salaries, etc.) | 3.3 (2/63) | 7.1 (6/84) | 5.8 (4/69) | 8.3 (1/12) | 5.7 (2/35) | 11.8 (10/85) | 10.5 (4/38) |

**TABLE 9** Responses to Question 1 According to Directorate (continued)

Question 1: What are the most significant issues/challenges/opportunities facing women scientists today as they plan their careers?

| CATEGORIES | SBE % OF | RESPONSES | MPS % OF | RESPONSES | ENG % OF | RESPONSES | EHR[a] % OF | RESPONSES | CISE % OF | RESPONSES | BIO % OF | RESPONSES | GEO % OF | RESPONSES |
|---|---|---|---|---|---|---|---|---|---|---|---|---|---|---|
| 8 Networking | 1.6 | (1/63) | 1.2 | (1/84) | 0 | (0/69) | 8.3 | (1/12) | 5.7 | (2/35) | 2.4 | (2/85) | 5.3 | (2/38) |
| 9 Affirmative action backlash/discrimination | 7.9 | (5/63) | 6.0 | (5/84) | 15.9 | (11/69) | 8.3 | (1/12) | 20.0 | (7/35) | 11.8 | (10/85) | 23.7 | (9/38) |
| 10 Positive: active recruitment of women/more opportunities | 7.9 | (5/63) | 15.5 | (13/84) | 13.0 | (9/69) | 8.3 | (1/12) | 8.6 | (3/35) | 3.5 | (3/85) | 15.8 | (6/38) |
| 11 Establishing independence | 3.3 | (2/63) | 4.8 | (4/84) | 1.4 | (1/69) | 0 | (0/12) | 2.9 | (1/35) | 3.5 | (3/85) | 0 | (0/38) |
| 12 Negative social images | 1.6 | (1/63) | 2.4 | (2/84) | 2.9 | (2/69) | 0 | (0/12) | 5.7 | (2/35) | 2.4 | (2/85) | 0 | (0/38) |
| 13 Trouble gaining access to nonacademic positions | 1.6 | (1/63) | 2.4 | (2/84) | 0 | (0/69) | 0 | (0/12) | 5.7 | (2/35) | 1.2 | (1/85) | 0 | (0/38) |
| 14 Sexual harassment | 3.3 | (2/63) | 1.2 | (1/84) | 0 | (0/69) | 0 | (0/12) | 5.7 | (2/35) | 0 | (0/85) | 2.6 | (1/38) |
| 15 No answer | 4.8 | (3/63) | 0 | (0/84) | 1.4 | (1/69) | 0 | (0/12) | 0 | (0/35) | 0 | (0/85) | 0 | (0/38) |
| 16 Cutthroat competition | 0 | (0/63) | 0 | (0/84) | 0 | (0/69) | 0 | (0/12) | 2.9 | (1/35) | 1.2 | (1/85) | 2.6 | (1/38) |

[a]Because of the low numbers of awardees, the EHR directorate should be carefully interpreted here. Many of the women representing this directorate have other disciplinary training and could be classified in other directorates. We have chosen not to interpret the EHR responses as a result.

**TABLE 10** Categorization of All Responses to Question 1 Across Directorates

Question 1: What are the most significant issues/challenges/opportunities facing women scientists today as they plan their careers?

| | CATEGORIES | RESPONSE NUMBERS[a] | MEANS OF RESPONSES (%) | | | | | | |
|---|---|---|---|---|---|---|---|---|---|
| | | | SBE | MPS | ENG | EHR | CISE | BIO | GEO |
| A | Pressures women face in balancing career and family | 1, 5, 7 | 26.0 | 37.7 | 28.0 | 38.9 | 29.5 | 35.3 | 35.1 |
| B[b] | Problems faced by women because of their low numbers and stereotypes held by others regarding gender | 3, 4, 8, 10, 12 | 10.5 | 10.2 | 12.4 | 15.0 | 16.6 | 9.0 | 14.8 |
| C[b] | Issues faced by both men and women scientists and engineers in the current environment of tight resources, which may pose particular difficulties for women | 2, 6, 16 | 6.8 | 6.7 | 6.8 | 0 | 8.6 | 7.4 | 11.4 |
| D | More overt discrimination and harassment | 9, 11, 13, 14 | 4.0 | 3.6 | 4.3 | 2.1 | 8.6 | 4.1 | 6.6 |

[a]Given the responses from all 4 years, after receiving faculty comments at various presentations of this research, and after working with the data, we exchanged two questions from categories B and D to better reflect the response groupings. Specifically, responses 10 and 12 (considered in category D in Rosser & Zieseniss, 2000) were moved to category B. Similarly, responses 11 and 13 (included in category B in Rosser & Zieseniss, 2000) were placed in category D.
[b]The alphabetic designation for categories B and C have been exchanged, compared with earlier papers (Rosser and Zieseniss, 2000) to present descending response percentages.

In my discipline [psychology], the laboratory climate is no different for men than for women. I can't think of a single area which one might consider an all male bastion. One problem, however, is the underrepresentation of women as journal editors and reviewers. I do not believe that male reviewers are biased. The problem is that these prestigious positions do help advance the careers and visibility of the incumbents. I don't know if women have failed to nominate themselves for these roles or if they won't take the job when offered. For whatever reasons, I think we need more women represented on publication boards. (1998 respondent 54)

There is a pecking order among the various subdisciplines within any particular field. For instance, in the general area of materials, there is applied science, fundamental colloid science, polymer chemistry, polymer physics, applied polymer science and engineering, cell biology, cellular biophysics, etc. It was actually a male colleague who observed that the subfield traditionally ... and those with the most women wind up on the bottom.

Consider the male-dominated biophysics arena ... compared with more traditional biology. Biophysicists impart a certain snobbery over pure biologists. Biophysicists also look down on the general field of polymers, but have more respect for certain subfields in complex fluids and polymer physics, which are more male dominated.

I certainly experienced some of this and observed more of it during my sabbatical time. But it is a huge help to attempt to continually inject women into the male dominated subfields to iron out all the snobbery. It really is there. One biophysicist told me that the ACS [American Chemical Society] journal *Macromolecules* was a low impact place to publish, and not worth it. But *Macromolecules* is the premier polymer journal. I publish there all the time. There is no better alternative for the polymers field. (1999 respondent 45)

My field of science [geophysics] is dominated by men and I feel isolated and at times depressed by the lack of possibility to socialize with other women at work, at meetings and conferences, or at the college social events. (1998 respondent 55)

In computer science it is common to sit in front of a screen in isolation and work for hours on end. I think that interferes with the kind of interaction that is necessary for professional development.

It is easy to retreat to your machine if you are uncomfortable with your colleagues. This may be true for men as well as women, but I suspect the lack of networking is more detrimental to women. (1997 respondent 11)

Contrary to expectations, the higher frequency of affirmative action/ backlash discrimination (response 9) and positive, active recruitment of women/more opportunities (response 10) did not always accompany a higher frequency of low numbers of women, isolation and lack of camaraderie/mentoring (response 3) within a particular directorate group. This suggests that perceptions of both negative discrimination and positive opportunities may not necessarily be correlated with low numbers in a field. This finding contradicts an earlier paper (see Rosser & Zieseniss, 2000) in which data from only the 1997 awardees were used to compare engineers with scientists.

The results of this questionnaire reveal that both women scientists and engineers found low numbers/lack of mentoring and gaining credibility/respect to be major issues. However, women engineers listed these issues more frequently than did their scientist colleagues. The women engineers also listed time management and learning the rules of the game to survive in a male-dominated environment as major difficulties.

These differences between women scientists and engineers appear to be directly related to the very small number of women engineers relative to the numbers of women scientists now present in many disciplines. Continuing low numbers provide particular challenges and some opportunities ... the low numbers that result in active recruitment of women into many areas of science, engineering, and mathematics have both positive and negative consequences. Demand in engineering and computer science gives women starting salaries that are equal to or higher than those of their male counterparts (Vetter, 1996). The recruitment can lead to various forms of backlash for a woman, ranging from overt discrimination to difficulties gaining credibility from peers and administrators who assume she obtained the position to fill a quota. (Rosser & Zieseniss, 2000, pp. 17–18)

Analysis of the data from the complete 4-year POWRE cohort does not support the conclusion drawn in the earlier paper (Rosser & Ziese-niss, 2000), which was based on the more limited data set. In the earlier study, the smaller numbers prohibited comparisons among directorates, so that engineers were compared with all other scientists grouped together, which may partially account for the discrepancy.

Table 11 presents the frequency of the first response for each category for question 1 for each awardee cohort by year. The data in Table 11 again reinforce that the first six responses, and for 1998, 1999, and 2000 awardees, affirmative action/backlash/discrimination (response 9) represent the most frequent responses. Table 12 shows the categorization of first response to question 1 across directorates. Note that when all responses are aggregated across directorates, the percentages are roughly proportional to the mean category responses across award year. However, when only first responses are categorized by directorate, CISE awardees have a lower mean response for category A and a higher mean response for category B. This may suggest that women in CISE perceive problems of their low numbers (response 3) to be of higher priority than the pressure to balance career and family (response 1), although both are important issues.

> Rather than attempting to speak for all disciplines, I'll speak only for my own — Computer Science. Among the most significant issues facing women Computer Scientists as they plan their careers is the recent decrease of women entering the field. The gap between numbers of men and women in the field had been narrowing, but now appears to be growing again. The isolation, lack of peer group, and resulting discomfort are issues for young women, much as they were 20 years ago. In the not very distant future, this will also translate into lack of role models for new female Computer Scientists. (1998 respondent 24)

Table 13 presents the frequency of the first response to question 1 by directorate of awardee, pooled over 4 years. Again, for most directorates, the first six responses plus response 9 (with the exception of MPS) or response 10 (in the case of MPS) are the most frequent.

TABLE 11 First Response to Question 1 by Year of POWRE Award

## Question 1: What are the most significant issues/challenges/opportunities facing women scientists today as they plan their careers?

| | CATEGORIES | 1997 % OF RESPONSES | (1997) | 1998 % OF RESPONSES | (1998) | 1999 % OF RESPONSES | (1999) | 2000 % OF RESPONSES | (2000) |
|---|---|---|---|---|---|---|---|---|---|
| 1 | Balancing work with family responsibilities (children, elderly relatives, etc.) | 46.3 | (31/67) | 60.5 | (72/119) | 54.1 | (53/98) | 46.7 | (49/105) |
| 2 | Time management/balancing committee responsibilities with research and teaching | 9.0 | (6/67) | 4.2 | (5/119) | 6.1 | (6/98) | 5.7 | (6/105) |
| 3 | Low numbers of women, isolation and lack of camaraderie/mentoring | 7.5 | (5/67) | 8.4 | (10/119) | 9.2 | (9/98) | 11.4 | (12/105) |
| 4 | Gaining credibility/respectability from peers and administrators | 7.5 | (5/67) | 5.9 | (7/119) | 3.1 | (3/98) | 9.5 | (10/105) |
| 5 | "Two career" problem (balance with spouse's career) | 7.5 | (5/67) | 2.5 | (3/119) | 8.2 | (8/98) | 7.6 | (8/105) |
| 6 | Lack of funding/inability to get funding | 7.5 | (5/67) | 1.7 | (2/119) | 4.1 | (4/98) | 3.9 | (4/105) |
| 7 | Job restrictions (location, salaries, etc.) | 1.5 | (1/67) | 5.0 | (6/119) | 2.0 | (2/98) | 0 | (0/105) |
| 8 | Networking | 3.0 | (2/67) | <1 | (1/119) | 0 | (0/98) | <1 | (1/105) |
| 9 | Affirmative action backlash/discrimination | 1.5 | (1/67) | 6.7 | (8/119) | 7.1 | (7/98) | 7.6 | (8/105) |
| 10 | Positive: active recruitment of women/more opportunities | 1.5 | (1/67) | <1 | (1/119) | 1.0 | (1/98) | 2.9 | (3/105) |
| 11 | Establishing independence | 1.5 | (1/67) | 0 | (0/119) | 3.1 | (3/98) | <1 | (1/105) |
| 12 | Negative social images | 3.0 | (2/67) | 1.7 | (2/119) | 1.0 | (1/98) | 0 | (0/105) |
| 13 | Trouble gaining access to nonacademic positions | 1.5 | (1/67) | <1 | (1/119) | 0 | (0/98) | <1 | (1/105) |
| 14 | Sexual harassment | 1.5 | (1/67) | 0 | (0/119) | 0 | (0/98) | 0 | (0/105) |
| 15 | No answer | 0 | (0/67) | <1 | (1/119) | 1.0 | (1/98) | 1.9 | (2/105) |
| 16 | Cutthroat competition | — | — | — | — | 1.0 | (1/98) | 0 | (0/105) |

**TABLE 12** Categorization of First Responses to Question 1 Across Directorates

Question 1: What are the most significant issues/challenges/opportunities facing women scientists today as they plan their careers?

| CATEGORIES | RESPONSE NUMBERS[a] | SBE | MPS | ENG | EHR | CISE | BIO | GEO |
|---|---|---|---|---|---|---|---|---|
| | | | | MEANS OF RESPONSES (%) | | | | |
| A  Pressures women face in balancing career and family | 1, 5, 7 | 19.1 | 23.8 | 20.3 | 22.2 | 12.4 | 21.2 | 20.2 |
| B[b]  Problems faced by women because of their low numbers and stereotypes held by others regarding gender | 3, 4, 8, 10, 12 | 3.5 | 3.6 | 4.3 | 6.7 | 7.4 | 2.6 | 3.1 |
| C[b]  Issues faced by both men and women scientists and engineers in the current environment of tight resources, which may pose particular difficulties for women | 2, 6, 16 | 3.7 | 2.4 | 2.4 | 0 | 2.9 | 4.3 | 5.3 |
| D  More overt discrimination and harassment | 9, 11, 13, 14 | 2.4 | 0.9 | 2.2 | 0 | 4.3 | 2.7 | 2.0 |

[a]Given the responses from all 4 years, after receiving faculty comments at various presentations of this research, and after working with the data, we exchanged two questions from categories B and D to better reflect the response groupings. Specifically, responses 10 and 12 (considered in category D in Rosser & Zieseniss, 2000) were moved to category B. Similarly, responses 11 and 13 (included in category B in Rosser & Zieseniss, 2000) were placed into category D.

[b]The alphabetic designation for categories B and C have been exchanged, compared with earlier papers (Rosser & Zieseniss, 2000) to present descending response percentages.

> I quit experimental physics for theoretical physics because I could not thrive in the down-and-dirty boy's world of the lab, complete with raucous and obscene humor, and virile competition for the best data. I am more comfortable in the computer lab and shops (wood, metal, electronics, etc.) at college and at home. My experimental skills, hand-eye coordination, and spatial aptitude are fine. My ability to josh around with the guys is limited. (1998 respondent 117)

Table 14 shows the responses to Question 2 when the data from all four years are pooled and categorized by NSF directorate of the awardee. As with Question 1, the most striking finding is the similarity of responses among the awardees from different directorates. However, some differences in responses emerge, which might be predicted, based upon the discipline. (Note that for this analysis education and human resources [EHR] is removed, since the numbers are small and the awardees come from different disciplinary backgrounds.) For example, large numbers of awardees from social, behavioral, and economic sciences (SBE) and CISE indicate that they are not in lab atmosphere/ can't answer (response 4) or give no answer (response 9). Some responses seem peculiar, or even contradictory. For example, awardees from engineering (ENG) give the highest response rates both to have not experienced problems (response 3) and to hostile environment/ intimidating/lack of authority (response 7). MPS awardees give high response rates to lack of camaraderie/communications and isolation (response 5) and to lack of numbers/networking (response 11). Although this response to question 2 is internally consistent, it contradicts the response of MPS awardees to question 1, where they gave a relatively low response rate to low numbers of women, isolation and lack of camaraderie/mentoring (see Table 9, response 3). Perhaps, as the following quotation would indicate, the issues become exacerbated with increasing ranks of the academic hierarchy.

> As a woman full professor of physics, I have found that the climate becomes more alienating as one advances in the career. In my experience there is now institutional support for junior faculty, but as one advances in the career, one finds that the number of women keeps decreasing, making it very lonely for more senior women.

**TABLE 13** First Response to Question 1 according to Directorate

## Question 1: What are the most significant issues/challenges/opportunities facing women scientists today as they plan their careers?

| CATEGORIES | SBE % OF RESPONSES | MPS % OF RESPONSES | ENG % OF RESPONSES | EHR[a] % OF RESPONSES | CISE % OF RESPONSES | BIO % OF RESPONSES | GEO % OF RESPONSES |
| --- | --- | --- | --- | --- | --- | --- | --- |
| (RESPONSES) | 50.8 (32/63) | 60.7 (51/84) | 50.7 (35/69) | 58.3 (7/12) | 31.4 (11/35) | 57.6 (49/85) | 50.0 (19/38) |
| 1 Balancing work with family responsibilities (children, elderly relatives, etc.) | 6.3 (4/63) | 4.8 (4/84) | 4.3 (3/69) | 0 (0/12) | 5.7 (2/35) | 7.1 (6/85) | 10.5 (4/38) |
| 2 Time management/balancing committee responsibilities with research and teaching | 11.1 (7/63) | 2.4 (2/84) | 11.6 (8/69) | 16.7 (2/12) | 17.1 (6/35) | 7.1 (6/85) | 10.5 (4/38) |
| 3 Low numbers of women, isolation and lack of camaraderie/mentoring | 3.2 (2/63) | 9.5 (8/84) | 7.2 (5/69) | 8.3 (1/12) | 14.3 (5/35) | 3.5 (3/85) | 2.6 (1/38) |
| 4 Gaining credibility/respectability from peers and administrators | 4.8 (3/63) | 10.7 (9/84) | 7.2 (5/69) | 8.3 (1/12) | 5.7 (2/35) | 1.2 (1/85) | 7.9 (3/38) |
| 5 "Two career" problem (balance with spouse's career) | 4.8 (3/63) | 2.4 (2/84) | 2.9 (2/69) | 0 (0/12) | 2.9 (1/35) | 5.9 (5/85) | 5.3 (2/38) |
| 6 Lack of funding/inability to get funding | 4.8 (3/63) | 0 (0/84) | 2.9 (2/69) | 0 (0/12) | 0 (0/35) | 4.7 (4/85) | 2.6 (1/38) |
| 7 Job restrictions (location, salaries, etc.) | 1.6 (1/63) | 1.2 (1/84) | 0 (0/69) | 0 (0/12) | 2.9 (1/35) | 0 (0/85) | 2.6 (1/38) |
| 8 Networking | 1.6 (1/63) | 0 (0/84) | 8.7 (6/69) | 0 (0/12) | 14.3 (5/35) | 8.2 (7/85) | 7.9 (3/38) |
| 9 Affirmative action backlash/discrimination | 4.8 (3/63) | 0 (0/84) | 0 (0/69) | 0 (0/12) | 2.9 (1/35) | 1.2 (1/85) | 0 (0/38) |
| 10 Positive: active recruitment of women/more opportunities | 0 (0/63) | 3.6 (3/84) | 0 (0/69) | 8.3 (1/12) | 2.9 (1/35) | 1.2 (1/85) | 0 (0/38) |
| 11 Establishing independence | 3.2 (2/63) | 1.2 (1/84) | 0 (0/69) | 0 (0/12) | 2.9 (1/35) | 1.2 (1/85) | 0 (0/38) |
| 12 Negative social images | 1.6 (1/63) | 1.2 (1/84) | 2.9 (2/69) | 0 (0/12) | 0 (0/35) | 1.2 (1/85) | 0 (0/38) |
| 13 Trouble gaining access to nonacademic positions | 1.6 (1/63) | 1.2 (1/84) | 0 (0/69) | 0 (0/12) | 0 (0/35) | 0 (0/85) | 0 (0/38) |
| 14 Sexual harassment | 0 (0/63) | 1.2 (1/84) | 1.4 (1/69) | 0 (0/12) | 0 (0/35) | 0 (0/85) | 0 (0/38) |
| 15 No answer | 4.8 (3/63) | 0 (0/84) | 0 (0/69) | 0 (0/12) | 0 (0/35) | 0 (0/85) | 0 (0/38) |
| 16 Cutthroat competition | 0 (0/63) | 0 (0/84) | 0 (0/69) | 0 (0/12) | 0 (0/35) | 0 (0/85) | 0 (1/38) |

[a]Because of the low numbers of awardees, the EHR directorate should be carefully interpreted here. Many of the women representing this directorate have other disciplinary training and could be classified in other directorates. We have chosen not to interpret the EHR responses as a result.

**TABLE 14** Responses to Question 2 According to Directorate

Question 2: How does the laboratory climate (or its equivalent in your subdiscipline) impact upon the careers of women scientists?

| CATEGORIES | SBE % OF | RESPONSES | MPS % OF | RESPONSES | ENG % OF | RESPONSES | EHR[a] % OF | RESPONSES | CISE % OF | RESPONSES | BIO % OF | RESPONSES | GEO % OF | RESPONSES |
|---|---|---|---|---|---|---|---|---|---|---|---|---|---|---|
| 1 Don't know/question unclear | 9.5 | (6/63) | 6.0 | (5/84) | 10.1 | (7/69) | 8.3 | (1/12) | 5.7 | (2/35) | 7.1 | (6/85) | 5.3 | (2/38) |
| 2 Balancing career and family/time away from home | 11.1 | (7/63) | 14.3 | (12/84) | 10.1 | (7/69) | 16.7 | (2/12) | 8.6 | (3/35) | 28.2 | (24/85) | 18.4 | (7/38) |
| 3 Have not experienced problems | 14.3 | (9/63) | 7.1 | (6/84) | 18.8 | (13/69) | 8.3 | (1/12) | 11.4 | (4/35) | 8.2 | (7/85) | 18.4 | (7/38) |
| 4 Not in lab atmosphere/can't answer | 19.0 | (12/63) | 4.8 | (4/84) | 1.4 | (1/69) | 8.3 | (1/12) | 17.1 | (6/35) | 0 | (0/85) | 2.6 | (1/38) |
| 5 Lack of camaraderie/communications and isolation | 4.8 | (3/63) | 20.2 | (17/84) | 11.6 | (8/69) | 33.3 | (4/12) | 5.7 | (2/35) | 9.4 | (8/85) | 5.3 | (2/38) |
| 6 "Boy's club" atmosphere | 7.9 | (5/63) | 14.3 | (12/84) | 10.1 | (7/69) | 25.0 | (3/12) | 8.6 | (3/35) | 12.9 | (11/85) | 10.5 | (4/38) |
| 7 Hostile environment/intimidating/lack of authority | 4.8 | (3/63) | 16.7 | (14/84) | 18.8 | (13/69) | 0 | (0/12) | 14.3 | (5/35) | 11.8 | (10/85) | 5.3 | (2/38) |
| 8 Establishing respectability/credibility | 9.5 | (6/63) | 9.5 | (8/84) | 72 | (5/69) | 8.3 | (1/12) | 8.6 | (3/35) | 8.2 | (7/85) | 5.3 | (2/38) |
| 9 No answer | 11.1 | (7/63) | 3.6 | (3/84) | 4.3 | (3/69) | 8.3 | (1/12) | 11.4 | (4/35) | 1.2 | (1/85) | 0 | (0/38) |
| 10 Positive impact | 3.2 | (2/63) | 6.0 | (5/84) | 72 | (5/69) | 16.7 | (2/12) | 2.9 | (1/35) | 12.9 | (11/85) | 21.1 | (8/38) |
| 11 Lack of numbering/networking | 7.9 | (5/63) | 11.9 | (10/84) | 5.8 | (4/69) | 8.3 | (1/12) | 2.9 | (1/35) | 7.1 | (6/85) | 0 | (0/38) |
| 12 General problem with time management | 1.6 | (1/63) | 3.6 | (3/84) | 29 | (2/69) | 0 | (0/12) | 5.7 | (2/35) | 5.9 | (5/85) | 2.6 | (1/38) |
| 13 Safety concerns/presence of toxic substances (health concerns) | 1.6 | (1/63) | 3.6 | (3/84) | 29 | (2/69) | 0 | (0/12) | 0 | (0/35) | 2.4 | (2/85) | 0 | (0/38) |
| 14 Benefit by working with peers | 4.8 | (3/63) | 1.2 | (1/84) | 29 | (2/69) | 0 | (0/12) | 2.9 | (1/35) | 4.7 | (4/85) | 7.9 | (3/38) |
| 15 Problem of wanting research independence | 1.6 | (1/63) | 0 | (0/84) | 14 | (1/69) | 0 | (0/12) | 0 | (0/35) | 1.2 | (1/85) | 2.6 | (1/38) |
| 16 Lack of funding | 0 | (0/63) | 1.2 | (1/84) | 0 | (0/69) | 0 | (0/12) | 0 | (0/35) | 3.5 | (3/85) | 10.5 | (4/38) |

**TABLE 14** Responses to Question 2 According to Directorate (continued)

Question 2: How does the laboratory climate (or its equivalent in your subdiscipline) impact upon the careers of women scientists?

| CATEGORIES | SBE % OF RESPONSES | MPS % OF RESPONSES | ENG % OF RESPONSES | EHR[a] % OF RESPONSES | CISE % OF RESPONSES | BIO % OF RESPONSES | GEO % OF RESPONSES |
|---|---|---|---|---|---|---|---|
| 17 Benefit from time flexibility/determine own lab hours | 3.2 (2/63) | 1.2 (1/84) | 1.4 (1/69) | 0 (0/12) | 0 (0/35) | 3.5 (3/85) | 5.3 (2/38) |
| 18 Did not answer | 0 (0/63) | 2.4 (2/84) | 1.4 (1/69) | 0 (0/12) | 0 (0/35) | 0 (0/85) | 0 (0/38) |
| 19 Department doesn't understand basic issues | 0 (0/63) | 1.2 (1/84) | 0 (0/69) | 0 (0/12) | 0 (0/35) | 0 (0/85) | 0 (0/38) |
| 20 Cultural/national stereotypes for women | 1.6 (1/63) | 2.4 (2/84) | 1.4 (1/69) | 0 (0/12) | 5.7 (2/35) | 1.2 (1/85) | 0 (0/38) |
| 21 Space | 1.6 (1/63) | 0 (0/84) | 0 (0/69) | 0 (0/12) | 0 (0/35) | 0 (0/85) | 0 (0/38) |
| 22 Better bathroom facilities | 0 (0/63) | 1.2 (1/84) | 0 (0/69) | 0 (0/12) | 0 (0/35) | 0 (0/85) | 0 (0/38) |

[a] Because of the low numbers of awardees, the EHR directorate should be carefully interpreted here. Many of the women representing this directorate have other disciplinary training and could be classified in other directorates. We have chosen not to interpret the EHR responses as a result.

Furthermore often family responsibilities make it still difficult for senior women to travel so that they often do not seem to acquire the same visibility as the peer male colleagues. The recent study carried out at MIT indeed points out some of the same problems. (1998 respondent 62)

My field of reproductive biology has always been very inclusive of females. Part of this stems from the whole field being somewhat disrespected for quite a long time, thus, "forcing" an early collaboration; part of it stems from the nature of our interests and the fact that more females entered this field earlier so that the adjustment has been going on for a longer period of time. I also feel that laboratory climate is segregated by generation. People of my generation have not experienced the level of sex discrimination that our colleagues perhaps only a decade older have. What I've seen is that I get along fine with everyone as I've no prehistory of battles, whereas some of my older female colleagues are perhaps more wary and are quicker to blame problems on a climate of discrimination. If anything, being female at this point gives you an edge because there seems to be a very sincere effort to get junior females into the ranks. (1998 respondent 70)

Anecdotal evidence suggests that many of the junior male scientists share child care, have professional spouses/partners, and want to have "a life" outside of the laboratory. Some of their expressions of problems with the culture of science and engineering appear similar to those of women. Whether these men will retain these attitudes as they advance through the ranks and whether the relatively larger percentages of women at the lower ranks will progress through the hierarchy without the increased attrition experienced by their predecessors remain to be seen.

Table 15 presents the frequency of the first response for each category for question 2. With a few notable exceptions (response 4 for 1999 and response 14 for 2000), overall, the responses are more evenly distributed among the first 12 categories during all 4 years than they were for question 1.

Table 16, which sorts the frequency of first responses by the directorate of awardee and pools them over the four years, reveals more

**TABLE 15** First Response to Question 2 by Year of POWRE Award

Question 2: How does the laboratory climate (or its equivalent in your subdiscipline) impact upon the careers of women scientists?

| CATEGORIES | 1997 % OF RESPONSES | RESPONSES | 1998 % OF REPSONSES | RESPONSES | 1999 % OF RESPONSES | RESPONSES | 2000 % OF RESPONSES | RESPONSES |
|---|---|---|---|---|---|---|---|---|
| 1 Don't know/question unclear | 16.4 | (11/67) | 4.2 | (5/119) | 6.1 | (6/98) | 5.7 | (6/105) |
| 2 Balancing career and family/time away from home | 9.0 | (6/67) | 11.8 | (14/119) | 10.2 | (10/98) | 11.4 | (12/105) |
| 3 Have not experienced problems | 11.9 | (8/67) | 16.8 | (20/119) | 10.2 | (10/98) | 9.5 | (10/105) |
| 4 Not in lab atmosphere/can't answer | 11.9 | (8/67) | 5.9 | (7/119) | 1.0 | (1/98) | 8.6 | (9/105) |
| 5 Lack of camaraderie/communications and isolation | 4.5 | (3/67) | 10.1 | (12/119) | 7.1 | (7/98) | 13.3 | (14/105) |
| 6 "Boy's club" atmosphere | 7.5 | (5/67) | 9.2 | (11/119) | 13.3 | (13/98) | 6.7 | (7/105) |
| 7 Hostile environment/intimidating/lack of authority | 6.0 | (4/67) | 11.8 | (14/119) | 13.3 | (13/98) | 7.6 | (8/105) |
| 8 Establishing respectability/credibility | 9.0 | (6/67) | 6.7 | (8/119) | 5.1 | (5/98) | 1.9 | (2/105) |
| 9 No answer | 7.5 | (5/67) | 6.7 | (8/119) | 5.1 | (5/98) | < 1 | (1/105) |
| 10 Positive impact | 4.5 | (3/67) | 6.7 | (8/119) | 6.1 | (6/98) | 10.5 | (11/105) |
| 11 Lack of numbering/networking | 1.5 | (1/67) | 4.2 | (5/119) | 6.1 | (6/98) | 4.8 | (5/105) |
| 12 General problem with time management | 1.5 | (1/67) | 1.7 | (2/119) | 4.1 | (4/98) | 3.8 | (4/105) |
| 13 Safety concerns/presence of toxic substances (health concerns) | 3.0 | (2/67) | — | — | 3.1 | (3/98) | 1.9 | (2/105) |
| 14 Benefit by working with peers | 1.5 | (1/67) | 1.7 | (2/119) | 1.0 | (1/98) | 4.8 | (5/105) |
| 15 Problem of wanting research independence | 1.5 | (1/67) | — | — | 1.0 | (1/98) | — | (0/105) |
| 16 Lack of funding | 0 | (0/67) | < 1 | (1/119) | 2.0 | (2/98) | < 1 | (1/105) |
| 17 Benefit from time flexibility/determine own lab hours | 1.5 | (1/67) | 1.7 | (2/119) | 2.0 | (2/98) | 1.9 | (2/105) |
| 18 Did not answer | — | | — | | 3.1 | (3/98) | — | |
| 19 Department doesn't understand basic issues | — | | — | | — | | — | |
| 20 Cultural/national stereotypes for women | — | | — | | — | | 4.8 | (5/105) |
| 21 Space | — | | — | | — | | — | |
| 22 Better bathroom facilities | — | | — | | — | | < 1 | (1/105) |

**TABLE 16** First Response to Question 2 According to Directorate

Question 2: How does the laboratory climate (or its equivalent in your subdiscipline) impact upon the careers of women scientists?

| CATEGORIES | SBE % OF RESPONSES | MPS % OF RESPONSES | ENG % OF RESPONSES | EHR[a] % OF RESPONSES | CISE % OF RESPONSES | BIO % OF RESPONSES | GEO % OF RESPONSES |
|---|---|---|---|---|---|---|---|
| 1 Don't know/question unclear | 9.5 (6/63) | 6.0 (5/84) | 8.7 (6/69) | 8.3 (1/12) | 5.7 (2/35) | 7.1 (6/85) | 5.3 (2/38) |
| 2 Balancing career and family/time away from home | 9.5 (6/63) | 7.1 (6/84) | 8.7 (6/69) | 16.7 (2/12) | 8.6 (3/35) | 17.6 (15/85) | 10.5 (4/38) |
| 3 Have not experienced problems | 14.3 (9/63) | 7.1 (6/84) | 18.8 (13/69) | 8.3 (1/12) | 11.4 (4/35) | 8.2 (7/85) | 18.4 (7/38) |
| 4 Not in lab atmosphere/can't answer | 19.0 (12/63) | 4.8 (4/84) | 1.4 (1/69) | 8.3 (1/12) | 17.1 (6/35) | 0 (0/85) | 2.6 (1/38) |
| 5 Lack of camaraderie/communications and isolation | 1.6 (1/63) | 16.7 (14/84) | 11.6 (8/69) | 25.0 (3/12) | 5.7 (2/35) | 7.1 (6/85) | 5.3 (2/38) |
| 6 "Boy's club" atmosphere | 7.9 (5/63) | 10.7 (9/84) | 7.2 (5/69) | 16.7 (2/12) | 8.6 (3/35) | 10.6 (9/85) | 7.9 (3/38) |
| 7 Hostile environment/intimidating/lack of authority | 4.8 (3/63) | 11.9 (10/84) | 14.5 (10/69) | 0 (0/12) | 11.4 (4/35) | 10.6 (9/85) | 5.3 (2/38) |
| 8 Establishing respectability/credibility | 3.2 (2/63) | 7.1 (6/84) | 7.2 (5/69) | 0 (0/12) | 2.9 (1/35) | 5.9 (5/85) | 2.6 (1/38) |
| 9 No answer | 11.1 (7/63) | 3.6 (3/84) | 4.3 (3/69) | 8.3 (1/12) | 11.4 (4/35) | 1.2 (1/85) | 0 (0/38) |
| 10 Positive impact | 3.2 (2/63) | 4.8 (4/84) | 4.3 (3/69) | 0 (0/12) | 2.9 (1/35) | 11.8 (10/85) | 21.1 (8/38) |
| 11 Lack of numbering/networking | 7.9 (5/63) | 6.0 (5/84) | 2.9 (2/69) | 8.3 (1/12) | 2.9 (1/35) | 3.5 (3/85) | 0 (0/38) |
| 12 General problem with time management | 0 (0/63) | 2.4 (2/84) | 1.4 (1/69) | 0 (0/12) | 5.7 (2/35) | 5.9 (5/85) | 2.6 (1/38) |
| 13 Safety concerns/presence of toxic substances (health concerns) | 0 (0/63) | 3.6 (3/84) | 2.9 (2/69) | 0 (0/12) | 0 (0/35) | 2.4 (2/85) | 0 (0/38) |
| 14 Benefit by working with peers | 4.8 (3/63) | 1.2 (1/84) | 1.4 (1/69) | 0 (0/12) | 2.9 (1/35) | 1.2 (1/85) | 5.3 (2/38) |
| 15 Problem of wanting research independence | 0 (0/63) | 0 (0/84) | 1.4 (1/69) | 0 (0/12) | 0 (0/35) | 0 (0/85) | 2.6 (1/38) |
| 16 Lack of funding | 0 (0/63) | 0 (0/84) | 0 (0/69) | 0 (0/12) | 0 (0/35) | 3.5 (3/85) | 2.6 (1/38) |

**TABLE 16** First Response to Question 2 According to Directorate (continued)

## Question 2: How does the laboratory climate (or its equivalent in your subdiscipline) impact upon the careers of women scientists?

| CATEGORIES | SBE % OF RESPONSES | MPS % OF RESPONSES | ENG % OF RESPONSES | EHR[a] % OF RESPONSES | CISE % OF RESPONSES | BIO % OF RESPONSES | GEO % OF RESPONSES |
|---|---|---|---|---|---|---|---|
| 17 Benefit from time flexibility/determine own lab hours | 1.6 (1/63) | 1.2 (1/84) | 1.4 (1/69) | 0 (0/12) | 0 (0/35) | 2.4 (2/85) | 5.3 (2/38) |
| 18 Did not answer | 0 (0/63) | 2.4 (2/84) | 1.4 (1/69) | 0 (0/12) | 0 (0/35) | 0 (0/85) | 0 (0/38) |
| 19 Department doesn't understand basic issues | 0 (0/63) | 0 (0/84) | 0 (0/69) | 0 (0/12) | 0 (0/35) | 0 (0/85) | 0 (0/38) |
| 20 Cultural/national stereotypes for women | 1.6 (1/63) | 2.4 (2/84) | 0 (0/69) | 0 (0/12) | 2.9 (1/35) | 1.2 (1/85) | 0 (0/38) |
| 21 Space | 0 (0/63) | 0 (0/84) | 0 (0/69) | 0 (0/12) | 0 (0/35) | 0 (0/85) | 0 (0/38) |
| 22 Better bathroom facilities | 0 (0/63) | 1.2 (1/84) | 0 (0/69) | 0 (0/12) | 0 (0/35) | 0 (0/85) | 0 (0/38) |

[a]Because of the low numbers of awardees, the EHR directorate should be carefully interpreted here. Many of the women representing this directorate have other disciplinary training and could be classified in other directorates. We have chosen not to interpret the EHR responses as a result

variation in responses to some categories by directorate. Not surprisingly, the results of Table 16 mirror closely those of Table 14. This mirroring reflects that the first response was often the sole response to question 2.

> I am not sure how to interpret this question. If you mean what is called the "culture," then there are still negative stereotypes (my example of a woman being offered a demeaning position which would not have been offered to a man would fit here). A group of women mathematicians is currently steaming about the fact that a well-known image used in the image-processing community turns out to be a playboy bunny centerfold of 30 years ago. I was startled myself when on a visit to a British university a couple of months ago I found myself in an academic atmosphere in which it was simply assumed that the standard person was male — as evidenced, for example, by a lack of women's restrooms in the math department. It made me realize how much things have changed here in the U.S. But I don't imagine that all traces of this stereotype have been eradicated. The damage they do may no longer be to keep women from achieving Ph.D.'s and planning careers, but I'm sure there is a negative effect of lowering women's expectations of the leadership roles they may assume. Fighting this nonsense every day takes it out of people, and keeps them from thinking about important things. (1999 respondent 4)
>
> It's especially difficult in the functional neuroimaging world to fit in as a woman. My "other" field, cognitive psychology, has enough senior women as role models that it's not as difficult to fit into the crowd. However, in neuroimaging, the climate doesn't feel particularly inviting or hospitable, and there are relatively few senior women who're leading this field. (2000 respondent 54)
>
> My personal experience has been quite positive, both in the university department where I work as well as in the field, observing at national telescope facilities. The climate certainly does impact women's careers, though. If one does not feel welcome, one may be less apt to continue on in that hostile environment. (2000 respondent 17)

Disciplinary and subdisciplinary differences in cultural environment combined with varying numbers of women become substantial factors that interact with laboratory climate to impact the lives of women scientists and engineers. Each of these factors interacts and intersects in diverse ways, as revealed in Chapter 5, and also varies with differing types of institutions.

Separation and examination of the intersection between gender and each other factor such as laboratory climate and discipline reveals considerable complexity in the lives of individual women scientists and engineers. Although the interviews and quotations provide hints of how factors such as age, marital status, race, disability, and nationality or origin impact their careers, these demographic data were not available to me for the POWRE awardees. Since the type of institution might have a significant impact on a career, I decided to ask the same questions to a different group of women scientists and engineers, primarily in small liberal arts colleges, since most of the POWRE awardees were concentrated in Research I and comprehensive institutions. The results are examined in the next chapter.

# CHAPTER 5
## THE DIFFERENCE AN INSTITUTION MAKES

### Susan Branton, Molecular Biologist

Susan Branton, looking back at age 53, believes that the reason she has been successful as a woman scientist is that she is stubborn and has stayed focused on doing research, rather than worrying about the status of the institution at which she would have a position. She consciously chose a position in a small, liberal arts college because of negative experiences she and colleagues had had at prestigious Research I institutions and large companies.

Because of an abusive advisor, she had a horrible experience as a graduate student at a prestigious Research I Midwestern public medical school. Although she ultimately received her Ph.D., she won one of the first sexual harassment suits filed in the 1970s to obtain it. Fortunately, she worked for a wonderful man at the NIH as a postdoc whose lab seemed like a paradise for scientists compared to her experience in graduate school.

When she finally went on the job market after 7 years as a postdoc, she scrutinized the institutions carefully to ensure that she did not land in another untenable situation. Susan believes that she dodged a bullet at a private Midwestern research institution where the biology department was grumbling about being under pressure to hire a woman. The position she turned down was accepted by the woman who brought a high-profile suit against the department in later years. Susan was pleased to accept a position at a small liberal arts college in the Northeast.

Somewhat reluctant to return to academia after the positive experience at NIH, receiving the CBL Professorship gave her confidence that someone would be watching out for her. She believes that the institution's awareness that someone with financial power would know if she were treated badly and denied tenure provided some insurance for her. She also received a POWRE award from NSF. Since all of her graduate students have been women, and since she has applied for grants for summer science camps for girls, as a CBL Professor she has attempted to attract other women to science.

Although she herself does not have children, Susan believes that child care becomes a significant barrier for women scientists, particularly because of the competition between the biological clock and the tenure clock. Other more subtle barriers such as those revealed in the MIT report result from men's perceptions that women deserve fewer resources in terms of space, start-up packages, support for and access to graduate students, and pay equity.

In her specific discipline of yeast molecular biology, the climate has improved dramatically. The older women are tough and watch out for the younger women. The relatively large number of women in the field results from the help and efforts of these women pioneers.

### Antoinette Johnson, Geologist

Antoinette Johnson entered a prestigious, private Midwestern liberal arts college thinking that she would not major in science. Although her scientist father had a large influence on her, especially since she was an only child, the professor in her geology class really motivated her to go into science. In addition to mentoring her and taking her out in the field, she felt that he took a personal interest in her. He was the one who persuaded her dad that taking some time off before pursuing a Ph.D. might be a good idea.

After 2 years of working at a desk from 9 to 5, Antoinette wanted to get her Ph.D. She shopped around, actively seeking programs with a higher percentage of women. Perceiving the top five places as male-dominated and too competitive, she did not apply to them. Although she was accepted at all four places where she applied, she went to the prestigious public research university in the Midwest because of the presence of women professors, the apparent happiness of the students, and the excellent fellowship she received.

Although she had a male advisor, the presence of a woman committed to studying women in science made her feel that the women in the program were watched after and that attention was paid to women's concerns. At the end of 4 years she had collected all of her data and had received a couple of rejections of attempted publications. She began to question her readiness to function as an independent scientist. Despite its negative repercussions for him, her advisor's suggestion that she do something else for a bit led her to obtain a Fulbright and go Down Under for a year.

Publishing the small project that she completed in New Zealand gave her the confidence to enter the job market upon her return, with only the first draft of her dissertation completed. From her 8–10 applications, two interviews at small liberal arts colleges resulted. The position offered by the private liberal arts institution for women was perfect for her. Although she was hired to replace a retiring senior woman, the department was mostly men. Her colleagues have supported her transition to work in a different area. Receiving an American Association of University Women [AAUW] Fellowship permitted her to have a full sabbatical year last year, resulting in her getting out the manuscripts and grant proposals that she needed to position her well for tenure.

Antoinette believes that the CBL Professorship has impacted her career positively, particularly with some of the older geologists where the title confers some degree of respect. Some of the younger men, however, appear jealous of the CBL, as well as the other opportunities such as the AAUW Fellowship for which her gender makes her eligible. She and the other three CBL professors hired at the same time keep track of each other and get together at least once each semester. Although being at a women's college makes them less isolated compared to many women faculty, the network they have formed provides particular support and the context that women science faculty need.

Antoinette can see improvements in the climate in geology since she began graduate school. Although a few sexist codgers make life difficult, the overwhelming majority of men go out of their way to be supportive of women geologists. The women geologists from different generations have looked out for her and tried to help her out. A major issue that academia must resolve for women scientists centers on the coincidence of the tenure clock with the biological clock. The unrealistic expectations for productivity and guilt associated with not devoting all of their time to the profession make it difficult for women to balance career and family.

At the dawn of the 21st century, following on the heels of the 1999 MIT report, the January 2001 statement by the presidents, chancellors, and provosts of the most prestigious institutions documenting institutional barriers for women scientists and engineers, and NSF's announcement of the ADVANCE initiative, rumblings of an undercurrent surfaced. Anecdotal reports that some women scientists actively choose to avoid research universities (Schneider, 2000) because of their hostile climate emerged. Supporting data documented that women make up 40% of tenure-track science faculty in undergraduate institutions (Curry, 2001), compared to less than 20% (NSF, 2000, table 5-15) at all 4-year colleges and universities.

In order to examine this trend and to understand some of the reasons behind the data and anecdotal reports, I decided to extend the e-mail questionnaire and interviews to women scientists and engineers concentrated at small liberal arts colleges. Although the NSF POWRE awardees included individuals from all types of institutions and at varying ranks, the overwhelming majority held the rank of untenured assistant professor and came from large Research I and comprehensive institutions.

Seeking a group of women scientists and engineers concentrated at small liberal arts colleges and private institutions who, like the POWRE awardees had received an externally validated prestigious award, I approached Jane Daniels, program director of the Clare Boothe Luce Professorships, given by the Henry Luce Foundation:

The Henry Luce Foundation, of which the Clare Boothe Luce Program is a major offering, was established in 1936 by the late Henry R. Luce, cofounder and editor-in-chief of Time Inc. With assets of $1 billion [in the year 2000], the Foundation supports programs focusing on higher education, East and Southeast Asia, American art, theology, public policy and the environment, and women in science and engineering .... The Clare Boothe Luce Program stands alone as the single most significant source of support for young women seeking to study or teach science, engineering, and mathematics. (Henry Luce Foundation, 2000, p. 2)

To this date, the program has made grants totaling $88.7 million to 1302 women, including 384 graduate fellowships, 781 undergraduate scholarships, and 4 fellowships to teachers. There have been 133 highly accomplished women in science, engineering, and mathematics appointed as Clare Boothe Luce professors in tenure track positions at 114 invited institutions and 14 designated colleges.

Dr. Jane Daniels generously provided access to the Clare Booth Luce (CBL) professors. She included the same e-mail questionnaire, with appropriate modifications, that I had sent to the POWRE awardees in her annual report information collected from the current CBL professors, as well as sending out the questionnaire to the former CBL professors. Forty-one of the 46 active CBL professors responded to the questionnaire; 8 of the 84 former CBL professors responded.

I then contacted a sub-sample of the questionnaire respondents with the "Request to Interview You" e-mail:

Recently you were kind enough to respond to a brief e-mail questionnaire sent to you by Jane Daniels as part of a research project related to your experiences as a CBL professor. As part of an ongoing effort to understand significant issues in the careers of women scientists and engineers, you are being asked to volunteer to participate in a research project as a follow-on to the e-mail questionnaire to which you responded. You have been selected as one of 15 volunteers to be interviewed from the respondents to the initial questions. Your responses will be compared and contrasted with a similar questionnaire responded to by the almost 400 NSF POWRE awardees and the interview responses of 25 volunteers from that group.

The project consists of one telephone interview lasting approximately 45 minutes with me, arranged via e-mail at a time that is mutually convenient for both you and me. During the interview you will be asked 5 questions exploring significant issues women scientists and engineers face in their careers and/or laboratories, as well as the impact that you perceive that receiving a CBL Professor award has had on your career. Up to 7 follow-on questions may be asked to clarify your responses to the 5 general questions.

Although this study has no known risks, you may refuse to respond to any question that you prefer not to answer for any reason. If you are harmed as a result of being in this study, please contact me. Neither the Principal Investigator (me) nor Georgia Institute of Technology have made provision for payment of costs associated with any injury resulting from participation in this study. All information concerning you obtained in the interview, as well as your responses to the previous questionnaire will be kept private. If information and quotations from your interview and/or questionnaire are published, you will be identified by number only and the information will be written in a way that maintains your confidentiality and prevents recognition of you individually. You will not be paid nor are there any costs to you by participating.

Your voluntary participation in this project is extremely important to shed light on issues important to the careers of women scientists and engineers. You may not benefit directly by participating in this study, but by underlining solutions, practices, and policies to attract and retain women in science and engineering; the results of this research should benefit institutions, funding agencies, and professional societies seeking to remove institutional barriers, policies, and practices that serve as obstacles for women scientists and engineers.

Please reply to this e-mail, indicating your willingness to participate in the interview. You may indicate times that would be especially convenient for the interview or I will request that information in a subsequent e-mail.

I would be happy to answer any questions you have about this project. Please contact me by e-mail or phone me at (xxx)xxx-xxxx for

answers to any questions. If you have questions about your rights as a
research subject please contact Alice Basler at (xxx)xxx-xxxx.
Thank you for your participation.
Sue V. Rosser, Dean and Professor

This resulted in my conducting telephone interviews, asking the
same five questions of the 11 CBL professors (10 current; 1 former) to
which the POWRE awardees responded.

Telephone Interview Questions
1. Tell me the story of your professional career, including the major
   influences, opportunities, and challenges that enabled you to
   become the woman scientist (engineer) you are today.
   Example follow-on/clarification: Since you suggest that you
   are an exception, what do you think are the most significant
   issues/challenges/opportunities facing women scientists today as
   they plan their careers?
2. How did receiving a Clare Boothe Luce Professorship award
   impact your career?
   Example follow-on clarification: Although it seems that the
   award was very positive for your career overall, did it have any
   negative impacts?
3. Do you think that the Clare Boothe Luce award you received
   helped to attract and retain other women in science?
   Example follow-on clarification: What other sorts of programs at your institution or others have you found to also be useful in attracting and retaining women in science (engineering)?
4. What are the key institutional barriers to women in science and
   engineering having successful academic careers?
   Example follow-on clarification: What solutions can institutions pursue to remove those barriers? Does your institution have
   an NSF ADVANCE award? If so, are you involved with
   ADVANCE.
5. What is the overall climate for women in your specific discipline?
   Example follow-on clarification: How does the laboratory climate (or its equivalent in your subdiscipline) impact upon the
   careers of women scientists?

As Table 17 documents, the CBL professors give very similar responses to those of the POWRE awardees to question 1 about the most significant issues, challenges, and opportunities facing women scientists and engineers as they plan their careers. Even more strongly than their POWRE awardee counterparts, the CBL professors found balancing career with family responsibilities (response 1) to be the most significant issue. The CBL professors also ranked low numbers of women, isolation, and lack of camaraderie (response 3) and the two-career problem (response 5) as significant issues, as had the POWRE awardees.

The responses of the CBL professors and POWRE awardees were remarkably similar with a few exceptions. CBL professors ranked time management/balancing committee responsibilities with research and teaching (response 2) much lower than did the POWRE awardees. In fact, only 1 of 41 current CBL professors mentioned this issue in the e-mail questionnaire responses. The likely reason that response 2 receives lower ranking from CBL professors than from POWRE awardees became evident from comments both in the e-mail questionnaire responses and in the interviews about the advantage of the flexibility of the CBL money that can be used to buy out teaching while establishing research, as well as for laboratory renovations, child care, travel, hiring students, and other needs.

> The most useful thing is the freedom to determine how to best spend the discretionary funds. I can use the funds to hire research assistants if needed without going through a lengthy proposal process. I can use the funds to buy myself some course release time so that I can spend more time on research and on mentoring female students. (respondent 26)
>
> The most useful aspects for me are the reduced teaching load and the research money. (respondent 36)

In her interview, Pat Vogue underlines the significance of this flexibility for her success:

## Pat Vogue, Biologist

Pat Vogue did not have brothers, so her father, a physicist, gave her substantial attention and encouraged her interest in science. Her mother, who believed strongly in women's liberation, assumed that Pat would have a career. Both parents gave her considerable freedom, such as allowing her to have animals in her room, to nurture her interest in biology.

At first when she entered college, she attempted to major in engineering. A fairly bad student at that point, she was pretty wild. She took time out from college and worked. When she went back, she attended a small school where the faculty gave her attention and supported her interest in biology.

After college she again worked, this time as a technician in a drosophila lab. The well-known drosophila geneticist for whom she worked encouraged her to go to graduate school. Blessed with an excellent Ph.D. advisor who led students to consider the bigger picture and ask broader questions, she thrived.

Pat believes that the CBL professorship made her research start much easier. The additional funds have given her the freedom to travel and to keep some folks who work in her lab employed. More significantly, it has freed up her grant money since she does not have to use it to reduce her teaching load and can apply it more directly to her research. The CBL Professorship may also have attracted better students to the program, since typically at the private university where she teaches, students receive teaching assistantships as support. The CBL graduate student fellowships permitted them to focus on their research immediately.

Although she had borne her children well before coming to this position, she still finds it a struggle to balance career and family. She thinks that a new policy that permits professors to request a 3-year extension, one year before coming up for tenure should be favorable for women.

Straddling two fields permits Pat to evaluate the climate for women in two different areas. Drosophila genetics has almost 50% women, and women hold leadership roles in conferences and symposia. In contrast the field of mammalian cell death remains male

**TABLE 17** Total Responses to Question 1

Question 1: What are the most significant issues/challenges/opportunities facing women scientists today as they plan their careers?

| CATEGORIES | 1997 % OF RESPONSES | 1998 % OF RESPONSES | 1999 % OF RESPONSES | 2000 % OF RESPONSES | CURRENT CBL PROFS. % OF RESPONSES | PAST CBL PROFS. % OF RESPONSES | TOTAL CBL PROFS. % OF RESPONSES |
|---|---|---|---|---|---|---|---|
| 1 Balancing work with family responsibilities (children, elderly relatives, etc.) | 62.7 (42/67) | 72.3 (86/119) | 77.6 (76/98) | 71.4 (75/105) | 73.2 (30/41) | 87.5 (7/8) | 75.5 (37/49) |
| 2 Time management/ balancing committee responsibilities with research and teaching | 22.4 (15/67) | 10.1 (12/119) | 13.3 (13/98) | 13.3 (14/105) | 0.1 (1/41) | 38.0 (3/8) | 8.2 (4/49) |
| 3 Low numbers of women, isolation and lack of camaraderie/mentoring | 23.9 (16/67) | 18.5 (22/119) | 18.4 (18/98) | 30.5 (33/105) | 26.8 (11/41) | — | 22.4 (11/49) |
| 4 Gaining credibility/ respectability from peers and administrators | 22.4 (15/67) | 17.6 (21/119) | 19.4 (19/98) | 21.9 (23/105) | 9.8 (4/41) | 12.5 (1/8) | 10.2 (5/49) |
| 5 "Two career" problem (balance with spouse's career) | 23.9 (16/67) | 10.9 (13/119) | 20.4 (20/98) | 20 (21/105) | 9.8 (4/41) | — | 8.2 (4/49) |
| 6 Lack of funding/inability to get funding | 7.5 (5/67) | 4.2 (5/119) | 10.2 (10/98) | •8.6 (9/105) | 4.9 (2/41) | 12.5 (1/8) | 6.1 (3/49) |
| 7 Job restrictions (location, salaries, etc.) | 9.0 (6/67) | 9.2 (11/119) | 7.1 (7/98) | 5.7 (6/105) | — | — | — |
| 8 Networking | 6.0 (4/67) | <1 (1/119) | — (0/98) | 4.8 (5/105) | 2.4 (1/41) | — | 2.0 (1/49) |
| 9 Affirmative action | 6.0 (4/67) | 15.1 (18/119) | 14.3 (14/98) | 12.4 (13/105) | 2.4 (1/41) | — | 2.0 (1/49) |

**TABLE 17** Total Responses to Question 1 (continued)

## Question 1: What are the most significant issues/challenges/opportunities facing women scientists today as they plan their careers?

| CATEGORIES | 1997 % OF RESPONSES | 1998 % OF RESPONSES | 1999 % OF RESPONSES | 2000 % OF RESPONSES | CURRENT CBL PROFS. % OF RESPONSES | PAST CBL PROFS. % OF RESPONSES | TOTAL CBL PROFS. % OF RESPONSES |
|---|---|---|---|---|---|---|---|
| 10 Positive; active recruitment of women/ more opportunities | 6.0 (4/67) | 10.1 (12/119) | 92 (9/98) | 14.3 (15/105) | 14.6 (6/41) | 12.5 (1/8) | 14.3 (7/49) |
| 11 Establishing independence | 3.0 (2/67) | — (0/119) | 61 (6/98) | 2.9 (3/105) | — | — | — |
| 12 Negative social images | 3.0 (2/67) | 3.4 (4/119) | 20 (2/98) | <1 (1/105) | 2.4 (1/41) | — | 2.0 (1/49) |
| 13 Trouble gaining access to nonacademic positions | 1.5 (1/67) | 1.7 (2/119) | 1.0 (1/98) | 1.0 (2/105) | — | — | — |
| 14 Sexual harassment | 1.5 (1/67) | <1 (1/119) | 20 (2/98) | 1.9 (2/105) | — | — | — |
| 15 No answer | — (0/67) | <1 (1/119) | 1.0 (1/98) | 1.9 (2/105) | — | — | — |
| 16 Cutthroat competition | — | — | 1.0 (1/98) | 1.9 (2/105) | — | 12.5 (1/8) | 2.0 (1/49) |
| 17 Gender bias in student evaluations | — | — | — | — | 2.4 (1/41) | 12.5 (1/8) | 4.1 (2/49) |

dominated, with few female speakers at meetings. Attending these two different meetings permits her to assess the substantial differences between a hospitable climate for women and a chilly environment.

CBL professors realized that buying out too many courses at a liberal arts institution, where teaching performance receives heavy emphasis in promotion and tenure decisions, might work against them in the tenure decision. Yet the 5-year commitment of the money and the relative flexibility of how it could be used came up repeatedly in e-mail and interview responses of the CBL professors as very positive features of the CBL professorship.

> Child care benefits — I've never heard of anything similar elsewhere, and it's really a great way to make it easier for women in academia to balance work and family (not that it's ever easy). (respondent 31)
>
> I like the money available for supplies and small equipment purchases and attending national meetings. It's very useful. (respondent 19)
>
> The fund given in addition to the academic salary has been very useful, especially since the things it could be put toward were left up to us (within reason). I have been able to use this fund to start a new project in the lab (that I had not accounted for in my start-up package), hire an undergraduate technician for the summer, and buy computer equipment that made my teaching duties easier. (respondent 4)

In contrast to the Clare Boothe Luce professors, a number of the POWRE awardees bemoaned the relatively small size of the grant, its short duration and relative inflexibility of funds.

In her interview, CBL professor Colleen Ivy particularly underlined this flexibility feature.

### Colleen Ivy, Mathematician

Colleen Ivy identified herself as good in math and science while in grade school and high school. The daughter of two Ph.D. scientists, a physicist father and biochemist mother, she naturally assumed that she would also pursue a Ph.D.

In college, she didn't really plan what her major would be. Eventually she realized that she had taken so much math that she might just as well major in it. After college, she took a year off before going to graduate school.

Very successful in graduate school, she received several prestigious fellowships. Near the end of the Ph.D., after completing her course work, she began to lose steam. She attributes this partially to less reinforcement, particularly since her advisor was Dutch and not voluble in his praise. Later, Colleen was amazed to learn that he considered her to be one of his best students.

Marrying another mathematics Ph.D. just before she finished her own Ph.D., they decided to move together, even if one of them didn't have the best situation professionally. Although both put their family first, at that point they moved to the West Coast where she received an excellent postdoc. After searching for jobs for a while, her husband left mathematics, changing careers to computer science. While there, she studied with her first woman role model and mentor, who also had a husband, child, and similar interests. That led Colleen to understand that unconsciously she had used her mother, who worked part time, as a role model. Because of her new mentor, Colleen realized that she could apply for full-time, tenure track positions.

Soon after she took the position at the small liberal arts college in New England, she had her first child; 2 years later she had the second. Originally both she and her husband worked full time, but now he stays at home with the children. Fortunately, the rural part of the state where they live opens the possibility of living on one salary.

The CBL Professorship gave Colleen flexibility to spend money on extra options such as laptops, professional memberships, and child care that made a difference in the quality of her life as a professional. She also hired women as research assistants, which provided opportunities for her to serve as a mentor to them.

With a five-course per year load, Colleen still finds balancing career and family as the biggest challenge for women scientists. Although it's possible to have a semester with pay at the birth of a child, strictures on having too many semesters with reduced loads before tenure make it difficult for women who have children during their pretenure phase. Child care near or on campus, especially for young children, also remains a challenge.

The climate for women in mathematics is generally good, although prominent speakers and symposium slots tend to be skewed toward men. Subtle bias in both professors' interpretations of females during interviews and student evaluations of female faculty may persist. Many faculty remain unaware of the extent to which deferential socialization of women leads to verbal nuances that interfere with the content of their presentations.

Gaining credibility/respectability from peers (response 4) constituted another difference in responses between CBL professors and POWRE awardees. Approximately 20% of all 4 years of POWRE awardees cited gaining credibility/respectability from peers and administrators (response 4) as a problem; while only about 10% of CBL professors cited this. Several of the POWRE awardees mentioned that since POWRE was an initiative for women only, many of their colleagues viewed the grant as less prestigious than other NSF grants, despite its very competitive success rate.

In contrast, many of the CBL professors underlined the named professorship as a factor that conferred prestige and respectability upon them, opening opportunities and doors, particularly with senior colleagues:

> The CBL Professorship is a tremendous help in two regards. First, simply the prestige of having a named professorship has been useful. Second, the financial security provided by this fellowship has allowed me to undertake risky projects in the lab. Since these are the type of projects that have the highest possible reward, this flexibility is greatly appreciated. (respondent 28)
>
> People take notice that I have a named chair. (respondent 2)

In her interview, Jessica Kimbel describes how the CBL opened doors at her own institution, as well as in the broader profession.

### Jessica Kimbel, Biologist

Jessica Kimbel believes that her mom deserves the credit for her becoming a scientist, since she encouraged her curiosity when she was young. A very good fourth-grade teacher who allowed her to clean out the science store room confirmed Jessica's interest in science, especially biology.

While in college at a Southern state university she worked in labs in the summer and became interested in research. Working in the labs of both men and women scientists provided her with role models of both genders. Although her male Ph.D. advisor at the private urban research institution in the Northeast where she pursued graduate work remained fairly distant, a strong accessible female member of her committee helped her substantially during her graduate work.

After receiving her Ph.D. she stayed in the urban area for a post-doc, primarily because of her boyfriend. Although she and her boyfriend broke up, the postdoc worked out well. She pursued a different approach than the one recommended by her postdoctoral advisor. He said "she ignored me and it worked," a very positive reaction to her science. Because she had obtained her own funding for her postdoc, she had more independence and flexibility to take risks.

After 5 years as a postdoc, she obtained a faculty position at a private doctoral institution in the same city and received the CBL Professorship. Married in 2000, she has received overwhelming support from the faculty and anticipates receiving tenure this year. Jessica believes that the CBL Professorship has gained her some recognition for her accomplishments and allowed her to stand out from her peers, since having a named professorship is relatively uncommon. For example, it affords her the opportunity to meet senior, distinguished faculty who are also invited to a series of annual dinners for all named chairs. She also attributes being asked to serve on the search committee for the dean of arts and sciences to the CBL Professorship.

Although she has women in her lab and teaches a developmental biology class where the women students often come to talk with her about career issues, she is uncertain that her position has led to the attraction of other women to science, especially at the undergraduate level. Keenly aware of the importance of senior women in science, she feels that she doesn't know enough about her institution to understand what barriers it presents for women in science and engineering. She has noted the presence of very few women in the upper administration, however.

Fortunately, on the national level, the climate in her small spe-
cialty of biology is quite positive for women. A few big labs dominate
the research; several of these are headed by well-established women
scientists. They serve as significant role models and have talked about
difficulties for women and how to help them.

The positive aspects of being a woman who receives more opportunities and was actively recruited emerge again in the differential
responses of POWRE awardees and CBL professors to positive; active
recruitment of women/more opportunities (response 10). Several CBL
professors indicated in both e-mail and interview responses their belief
that the CBL award had led to their recruitment and to positive attitudes of their colleagues and institution toward them and other women
in science.

> I appreciate the prestige associated with the award and the commit-
> ment it represents by the university to further women in science. The
> discretionary fund is also a very welcome element of the award.
> (respondent 25)
>     The most useful aspect of the CBL Professorship is the recogni-
> tion of Clare Booth Luce's contribution to women in society. Many
> parents of female students take comfort in hearing about my profes-
> sorship, and from this understand that women engineers are well
> accepted here. As well colleagues around the country either recognize
> her name, or learn about her contribution through this professorship.
> (respondent 11)

Both Morris and Van Hoek indicate in their interviews the very
different, but significant, positive opportunities that their gender and
the Clare Booth Luce Professorship have brought.

### Clarice Morris, Engineer

Clarice Morris knew that engineering provided a career option
because of the influence of her father who was an engineer. Good at
math and science in high school, she found that she particularly
enjoyed their practical applications.

When she entered a technological institution in the Northeast as an undergraduate, she liked it right away, feeling as if she fit in well and was good at engineering. Although she had thought only of becoming an engineer, the faculty encouraged her to go to graduate school.

While pursuing her MS at a large prestigious Midwestern state university, she became hooked on research. Because she had common research interests with a faculty member at a private research university in the Northeast, she transferred there to pursue her Ph.D. As she finished her Ph.D., she applied for a position in South Africa. She wanted to have some teaching experience, but she didn't want to lose being current in her field, despite her desire to avoid jumping right into the U.S. job market.

Even after receiving her Ph.D., she didn't really think of a long-term career in research. In many ways her decision to pursue an academic position sprang from her desire to prove that she could do it. In fact, she thought she would probably just get tenure to show that she could do it and then quit academia to become an engineer in industry.

While she was still in South Africa, the institution from which she received her undergraduate degree nominated Clarice for the CBL Professorship. She believes that receiving the professorship impacted her career considerably because it provided the start-up cushion to allow her to choose opportunities and pursue long-term, higher quality money rather than having to go after easy money to get her research started. Receiving an NSF Young Investigator award in her first year also removed considerable pressure and helped to launch her research successfully. She believes that the press coverage and prestige of the award may have led to invitations for her to speak at local high schools and junior high schools in the area.

Clarice thinks that the relative isolation of academic research, coupled with some subtle factors such as women being told that some of their success stems from their being a woman, despite slower rates of promotion, serves as a barrier for women. Problems implementing and interpreting policies, such as stopping the tenure clock to facilitate balancing work and family in equitable, appropriate ways, cause additional obstacles.

The overall climate for women in mechanical engineering remains difficult because of continuing small numbers. Being the only woman, or one of a very few, at a meeting makes her question whether she belongs in this field with all of these guys. Perceptions of the field may also deter, especially when parents and/or peers suggest that mechanical engineering is dirty and therefore inappropriate for women.

## Jan Van Hoek, Computer Scientist

Jan Van Hoek credits her parents, especially her father, for her interest in mathematics. Because he liked math and spent considerable time with her working through problems, she became a star math student. Her mother, a strong, independent career woman, also taught her to persevere. Her parents let her know that she could and should do anything she wanted so that she would not lose interest in math when the nuns in the Catholic school she attended did not track her into the honors math course for the first 2 years.

Because her father died during her senior year in high school, Jan worked for a year before going to college. Already married, she ended up with a degree in technical journalism because they didn't offer the third semester of calculus at the college where she took night classes. After receiving her first BA, she worked and took her second BS and her MS in engineering. While working for Bell Labs, she pursued her Ph.D. in computer science.

She believes that the CBL Professorship helped her to get her position, since the college recognized they would be likely to receive the professorship if they extended the position at the liberal arts college on the West Coast to her and nominated her for the award. The college has made considerable efforts to attract women. During the 4 years Jan has taught at the institution, the number of women computer science majors has gone from two to many.

Because having a critical mass of women becomes essential for retaining women, Jan has formed a social group of the five women faculty now in engineering. Although she grew up in the math and science world where she became accustomed to few women, no longer being the only woman in engineering makes life much easier.

She finds the atmosphere in computer science overall to be fairly positive for women and warmer than engineering, although the nerdy, geeky culture repels many women. Partly because it's a relatively new field, less time has been available for old boys' networks to develop. Women have made significant contributions to the short history of the field.

The Clare Booth Luce professors responded similarly (see Table 18) to the POWRE awardees to e-mail question 2: "How does the laboratory climate (or its equivalent in your subdiscipline) impact upon the careers of women scientists?" As with the POWRE awardee responses, the responses to question 2, in contrast to question 1, reflect less consensus. The response of the CBL professors for balancing career and family/time away from home (response 2) was even stronger (24.5%) than the primary response of the POWRE awardees across all years (15.6%). Somewhat fewer (2.0%) of the CBL professors than POWRE awardees (12.1%) indicated that they had not experienced any problems (response 3). More of the CBL professors than POWRE awardees indicated that they benefit by working with peers (response 14), but also that they face a hostile environment/intimidating/lack of authority (response 7). Because of the relatively small numbers of CBL professors, dividing the data by disciplines or into the five stages for laboratory climate analysis, as was done for the POWRE awardees, was not possible for the CBL professors.

As with question 1, the nuances of difference and context for the responses become clearer from the qualitative answers given by the CBL professors.

> Successful laboratory work often requires long blocks of time, which may often impinge on family time (if relevant) so that women who are primary caregivers for dependents have to work even more efficiently. Some constraints may also be imposed if the female scientist has other obligations. It is nearly impossible to successfully complete laboratory-based or field-based projects without being able to spend large blocks of time in the environment. When experiments are not successful, morale declines and motivation for the woman scientist may also decline. (respondent 39)

**TABLE 18** Total Responses to Question 2

Question 2: How does the laboratory climate (or its equivalent in your subdiscipline) impact upon the careers of women scientists?

| CATEGORIES | 1997 % OF RESPONSES | 1998 % OF RESPONSES | 1999 % OF RESPONSES | 2000 % OF RESPONSES | CURRENT CBL PROFS. % OF RESPONSES | PAST CBL PROFS. % OF RESPONSES | TOTAL CBL PROFS. % OF RESPONSES |
|---|---|---|---|---|---|---|---|
| 1 Don't know/Question unclear | 16.4 (11/67) | 4.2 (5/119) | 7.1 (7/98) | 5.7 (6/105) | 12.2 (5/41) | 12.5 (1/8) | 12.2 (6/49) |
| 2 Balancing career and family/time away from home | 13.4 (9/67) | 19.3 (23/119) | 16.3 (16/98) | 13.3 (14/105) | 26.8 (11/41) | 12.5 (1/8) | 24.5 (12/49) |
| 3 Have not experienced problems | 11.9 (8/67) | 16.8 (20/119) | 10.2 (10/98) | 9.5 (10/105) | 2.4 (1/41) | — | 2.0 (1/49) |
| 4 Not in lab atmosphere/can't answer | 11.9 (8/67) | 5.9 (7/119) | 1.0 (1/98) | 8.6 (9/105) | 2.4 (1/41) | 25.0 (2/8) | 6.1 (3/49) |
| 5 Lack of camaraderie/communications and isolation | 9.0 (6/67) | 11.8 (14/119) | 9.2 (9/98) | 14.3 (15/105) | 12.2 (5/41) | 12.5 (1/8) | 12.2 (6/49) |
| 6 "Boys' club" atmosphere | 9.0 (6/67) | 9.2 (11/119) | 18.4 (18/98) | 9.5 (10/105) | 12.2 (5/41) | — | 10.2 (5/49) |
| 7 Hostile environment/intimidating/lack of authority | 9.0 (6/67) | 14.3 (17/119) | 15.3 (15/98) | 8.6 (9/105) | 19.5 (8/41) | 12.5 (1/8) | 18.4 (9/49) |
| 8 Establishing respectability/credibility | 9.0 (6/67) | 10.9 (13/119) | 10.2 (10/98) | 3.8 (4/105) | — | 25.0 (2/8) | 4.1 (2/49) |
| 9 No answer | 7.5 (5/67) | 6.7 (8/119) | 5.1 (5/98) | <1 (1/105) | — | — | — |
| 10 Positive impact | 6.0 (4/67) | 10.1 (12/119) | 6.1 (6/98) | 11.4 (12/105) | 2.4 (1/41) | — | 2.0 (1/49) |
| 11 Lack of numbering/networking | 4.5 (3/67) | 6.7 (8/119) | 12.2 (12/98) | 4.8 (5/105) | 2.4 (1/41) | — | 2.0 (1/49) |
| 12 General problem with time management | 4.5 (3/67) | 1.7 (2/119) | 5.1 (5/98) | 3.8 (4/105) | — | 25.0 (2/8) | 4.1 (2/49) |
| 13 Safety concerns/presence of toxic substances (health concerns) | 3.0 (2/67) | — | 4.1 (4/98) | 1.9 (2/105) | 2.4 (1/41) | — | 2.0 (1/49) |
| 14 Benefit by working with peers | 3.0 (2/67) | 2.5 (3/119) | 3.1 (3/98) | 5.7 (6/105) | 14.6 (6/41) | 25 (2/8) | 16.3 (8/49) |

**TABLE 18** Total Responses to Question 2 (continued)

### Question 2: How does the laboratory climate (or its equivalent in your subdiscipline) impact upon the careers of women scientists?

| CATEGORIES | 1997 % OF RESPONSES | 1998 % OF RESPONSES | 1999 % OF RESPONSES | 2000 % OF RESPONSES | CURRENT CBL PROFS. % OF RESPONSES | PAST CBL PROFS. % OF RESPONSES | TOTAL CBL PROFS. % OF RESPONSES |
|---|---|---|---|---|---|---|---|
| 15 Problem of wanting research independence | 30 (2/67) | — | 1.0 (1/98) | <1 (1/105) | — | — | — |
| 16 Lack of funding | 15 (1/67) | <1 (1/119) | 51 (5/98) | <1 (1/105) | — | — | — |
| 17 Benefit from time flexibility/ determine own lab hours | 30 (2/67) | 17 (2/119) | 31 (3/98) | 19 (2/105) | 2.4 (1/41) | — | 2.0 (1/49) |
| 18 Did not answer | — | — | 31 (3/98) | 0 — | | | |
| 19 Department doesn't understand basic issues | — | — | — | <1 (1/105) | | | |
| 20 Cultural/national stereotypes for women | — | — | — | 67 (7/105) | | | |
| 21 Space | — | — | 1.0 (1/98) | — | | | |
| 22 Better bathroom facilities | — | — | — | <1 (1/105) | | | |

A practical reality of biochemistry is that, to be highly successful, the scientist must inevitably spend long hours in the lab. This is particularly difficulty for women who are trying to juggle small children with work. (respondent 28)

Here again, I think one of the main issues comes down to family. I know of several men who had children while in graduate school, but only one woman, and her baby was born when she was writing her thesis and effectively out of the lab. In competitive fields, a person who takes time off from work may be "scooped" and miss out on, or at least delay, a chance for career advancement. On a more immediate time scale, experimental work often demands large blocks of time which may be difficult to work into the schedule of someone with a family. In principle, this should affect men and women equally, but (at least anecdotally) women seem to be the ones to tend to their families at the expense of the laboratory work. This means that they may accomplish less than a man in the same time span, leading to lower productivity overall. This of course, negatively impacts the woman's career trajectory. Of course, not all women are affected in this negative way due to the personal choices they make, the nature of the work they do, and the policies and procedures of the individual laboratories in which they work. (respondent 13)

The responses from five CBL professors describe particularly well some of the reasons that women appear to benefit from collaboration compared to a more hostile, competitive environment fostered in many labs.

There are many different mentoring styles practiced in laboratory science. While each of them may represent a valid approach to teaching, I have found that women do not respond equally well to all of them. Specifically, I have had female graduate students come to me with problems they are facing in their respective laboratories, especially when the learning environment created there is highly competitive. Often the advisors in this case maintain a distance from their students and share their personal knowledge sparingly, yet praise and reward students who obtain knowledge independently. Some individuals thrive in such an environment that is designed to foster complete independence. Many women feel uncomfortable in such an environment and prefer a more cooperative way of learning with the free sharing of knowledge among all peers and between the advisor and the students. These women will often retreat from such an intense competitive environment, increasing their isolation and feelings of inadequacy. It is not uncommon for these women to eventually drop out of science altogether. (respondent 25)

My field is extremely competitive, and I believe that it is important to create an environment where beginning scientists can be introduced to the discipline and to the scientific process in a nurturing environment. Providing this nurturing, though challenging environment has the ultimate goal of allowing beginning scientists to recognize their own strengths and gain the confidence that will allow them to succeed in this field. I think that the aggressive nature of the field in general, a tone that has been historically created, tends to dissuade women from pursuing careers beyond the postdoctoral level. (respondent 32)

I am fortunate to have worked in laboratories where the environment was very stimulating and supportive. I know many, however, who have had less pleasant experiences. Some of my female peers have left laboratory research altogether because they found the competitiveness of larger laboratories too stressful to cope with. (respondent 31)

I think that this touches upon the same issues as above. The laboratory climate tends to be fiercely competitive, rewarding those who work the longest hours. This can put real pressure on women who have spouses and children to care for at home.

Physics labs also tend to be run along an aggressive model in which colleagues are encouraged to criticize each other's work, rather than to work constructively together. This can be completely demoralizing — I saw a lot of talented women wash out of my graduate program because they internalized the criticism of their fellow students. I'm not sure that there is much anyone can do about this, though, other than to resolve to create a more constructive climate in her own lab! (respondent 23)

An open and supportive laboratory climate is very important to the well-being of women scientists. Here at the college, I feel we have a very positive climate for women in our classroom and research laboratories. This is in part due to the high percentage of women in our science classes, reaching almost 70%. A sense of camaraderie often develops. Female students tell me that gender is really a non-issue in the laboratory setting. Doing field work, however, can bring up some gender issues/stereotypes. For example, for some female students it bothers them if male students are stronger and hence do some more of the field work (e.g., pounding in a soil corer) more quickly or apparently effortlessly. (respondent 9)

In her will, Clare Boothe Luce stipulated 13 colleges and universities, plus one private high school, to receive funding in perpetuity. The selection committee has only recently awarded CBL Professorships at several larger institutions, including the University of Washington, Stanford, the University of Maryland — College Park, and the California Institute of Technology. The smaller, private colleges where the Clare Boothe Luce professors concentrate can more easily provide this positive, nurturing environment for female students. Many of the Clare Boothe Luce professors emphasize the efforts they make to provide this supportive atmosphere in their labs.

Positively. The laboratory is a place where women can learn, challenge themselves, make mistakes, and work together in a community. (respondent 34)

The laboratory climate varies vastly. Clearly, in a rewarding or at least positive environment, any woman could envision a career doing research. It is my hope that the experiences my students have researching with me will be only positive. I want them to experience the excitement and potential fulfillment of this pursuit so that they might choose or at least consider it as a career for themselves. (respondent 20)

In her interview, Jana Jackson emphasizes the outreach she does to build the pipeline.

### Jana Jackson, Engineer

Jana Jackson credits her family as major influences that led her to become a scientist. As the fourth out of five siblings, she felt the challenge from her older siblings. Her sister, although not a scientist, became the only female water polo player. Tussling and wrestling with her two brothers encouraged her to become even more competitive.

Her father, a city planner for the USGS, probably influenced her decision to receive an MS in urban planning. When she was in the Peace Corps, he sent her notices about opportunities in transportation. Her mother, who was strong willed, also encouraged her in a technical direction.

When she was growing up, the family's move to the Bay Area, with its excellent public schools, provided her with great preparation for the prestigious state university. The faculty there took an interest in her and introduced her to other faculty, encouraging her even as an undergraduate to think about an academic career. Although she had no female mentors until she began teaching, she found that the male faculty both in undergraduate and graduate school did mentor her.

Receiving the nomination for the CBL Professorship before she started teaching, provided her with extra support crucial to her career. She uses the momentum from the award to attempt to improve the situation for younger women. Although Jana was not a member of the Society of Women Engineers (SWE) either as an undergraduate or when she began teaching, she fought to become the advisor of SWE. Since the organization already had two other advisors, she knew she had to be a role model and seek out the position. She undertakes considerable outreach, using the Expanding Your Horizons Program, the Girl Scouts, and Engineering Week to encourage middle school girls to consider careers in engineering. She has used some of the Luce money to sponsor a Friday Forum for Future Women Faculty.

Because the Luce money can be used flexibly, for child care expenses, administrative support, and for hiring assistants, it goes a long way toward removing institutional barriers that discourage women in science and engineering. Since academia, unlike industry, doesn't seem to be something that people can leave and then reenter, policies such as stopping the tenure clock for a year at the time of childbirth become crucial for retaining women. Most institutions will not permit women to take a cut in salary and work part time when their children are young; in Jana's opinion, that change would make a real difference.

Because the field of transportation is quite innovative, it has progressed beyond the more traditional boundaries of civil engineering and provides a very positive climate for women. Jana believes that she has received more opportunities than some of her male colleagues because of her gender. In addition to receiving the CBL, many male professors singled her out and provided support for her during her education. She thinks that NSF gives CAREER awards to women at earlier stages, which facilitates their careers, although it may make it less likely that they receive PECASE awards.

Annelise Swinton also talks about hiring women students for her lab.

### Annelise Swinton, Biologist

Annelise Swinton never had any female mentors, although all of her male mentors proved extremely supportive of women. Enduring the struggles that all women scientists experience was possible because her parents encouraged her to do what she wanted. Because she did well in school, the faculty pushed her toward becoming a physician. In college, she realized that she liked science but did not wish to become a physician.

An excellent professor and mentor invited her to work in his lab and sent her to Africa. The level of confidence that he demonstrated in her as an undergraduate encouraged her to go to graduate school. She attended a university in the Mid-south, working with an advisor that she met via her undergraduate mentor. He also went out of his way to support women and diversity, as well as to socialize individuals to the profession of physiology and endocrinology.

She obtained her first job at a private liberal arts institution in the Midwest right out of graduate school. For the first time, she enjoyed being in a department with more women than men. Although she liked the 5 years there, she jumped at the position at the private liberal arts institution in her home state in New England.

The CBL professorship has encouraged the institution to hire women in science. With only one tenured woman out of a science faculty of 40, the CBL influence seems critical to attracting and retaining women in science. Since she hires women students to work in her lab, it also encourages women undergraduates.

The absence of senior women in science to serve as mentors becomes a substantial barrier for junior women. This absence becomes further complicated by the dearth of women in senior administrative positions and holding endowed chairs. Few individuals in leadership positions understand the subtle aspects of gender bias, such as those that emerge from student evaluations of teaching, that may negatively impact women's salaries and standing. The overall climate for women in biology, however, has really improved because of increasing numbers of women and willingness to collaborate.

Although the small, private college with its emphasis on teaching may provide a more supportive atmosphere for women students, the notion that it provides more time and less pressure than the research institution for women faculty may be an illusion. Typically the teaching load in a small liberal arts college is higher than that in a Research I institution. The pressures and time demands of the types of institutions may differ, while remaining intense at both. For example, as suggested in the interview with Swinton, in institutions where teaching takes priority over research for promotion and tenure, as well as salary decisions, pressures erupt from subtle gender bias in teaching evaluations or negative perceptions from colleagues about too much course buyout. The expectations from smaller, private institutions for all faculty to attend parents' weekends, ceremonies, and other events may make time demands similar in amounts to those expected for faculty at Research I institutions to spend on secondary research-related activities.

Similarly, the absence of graduate students and postdocs at small liberal arts colleges means that faculty must prepare and teach all the laboratories, as well as the lecture courses. Faculty in these institutions must rely only on undergraduates in their research. Using undergraduates in research provides students with excellent experience, now documented as one of the most, if not the most, significant factor for attracting them to pursue graduate studies in science and technology.

However, undergraduate students do not and cannot further the research agenda of faculty in ways that technicians, graduate students, and postdocs found in laboratories of most Research I institutions can. This tends to decrease the research productivity of faculty in these institutions, as the quotations from the e-mail questionnaire suggest.

> I need technical assistance with my research so that I can supervise students and my own research program more effectively. I need to hire a technician, but the CBL program does not fund support staff. I am finding, as time goes on, that I cannot give my research and student advising the attention they deserve without some extra help with day-to-day running of laboratory and field operations. Most funding agencies do not support technical staff. (respondent 38)
>
> With our campus culture, it is difficult to make use of student stipends during the semester. Typically, a student who works for credit will be able to devote more hours to research than a student who works for pay. Funds allocated to a part-time technician would probably be more beneficial, both for me and for students doing independent study or honors projects. (respondent 7)
>
> Most problematic: The funds could be more flexible regarding international travel, student stipends, and general allocations. For example, I find that hiring students during the academic year is an inefficient use of funds; students become very busy, and they tend to focus instead on coursework or laboratory work for academic credit. That money could be better used if dedicated to research expenses, or if we were given flexibility in its use. (respondent 5)

Teresa Giuseppi underlines the importance of women faculty for attracting women graduate students.

### Teresa Giuseppi, Chemist

> Teresa Giuseppi met her husband while she was still an undergraduate and has been married for 16 years. After she received her MS and while her husband was working on his Ph.D., she worked as a master's level chemist for 4 years. This early exposure to the work world convinced her that she must obtain her Ph.D. Her boss, who came from India, held very traditional ideas about women and looked

down particularly on someone who only held the MS degree. He threatened her and told her to know her place.

Because she had already begun her family and her child was 9 months old, she chose to pursue her Ph.D. locally in the Midwestern city where her husband worked so they could cooperate on child care. Her graduate school experience and the mentoring she received were okay; she did not feel discrimination either for or against her. The only female professor in the department encouraged her to go into industry because of personal difficulties she had encountered with the glass ceiling in academia. During the last 2 years of graduate school, her husband took a position on the East Coast, so they had a commuter marriage. Since their son was with her the first of those years, she felt especially constrained in her work. During the second year, her husband took their son with him; this permitted her to work the long hours in the lab need to complete her Ph.D.

She sought a postdoc on the East Coast so that she and her husband could be together. Because she was geographically constricted, she remained in the postdoc for 5 years and was used by her boss to run the lab. The geographic constrictions and few academic positions available made her consider leaving the field.

Fortunately the position at the small liberal arts college in the Northeast emerged at just the right time. Teresa believes that the CBL Professorship provided the impetus for the department to hire her, since the school only had to pay start-up costs and no salary for the first 5 years. She only wishes that the professorship had provided enough money to hire a postdoc to help produce research results; however, she's grateful for the additional funds to supplement the minimal start-up provided by the institution.

She believes that the CBL is crucial for attracting other women to science, particularly at the graduate level. Although undergraduates now enter chemistry almost at the level of parity, this is less true at the graduate level. Women faculty should be the priority, as they are the key to attracting more women to the field.

Teresa believes that both academic institutions and the field of chemistry as a whole have improved for women. Having children still becomes a stigma, and a double standard seems to emerge for men with a family compared to women. Although she believes that attitudes are changing, some old boy approaches predominate in the culture of the discipline.

As the interview with Teresa Giuseppi indicates, the small liberal arts college does not necessarily provide the most conducive environment for a productive research career. The combination of higher teaching loads with the dearth of graduate students and postdocs means that faculty in these small liberal arts colleges often must prepare and teach the laboratory courses (a function typically carried out by graduate students in Research I institutions) as well as run their own research labs (a function often left to postdocs in Research I institutions). This combination often results in less time for writing grants, producing research results, and publication. Ultimately, the research slows or may stop entirely, since without funds, research in most science and engineering disciplines, unlike that in humanities and some areas of the social sciences, is not possible. This in turn has implications for maintaining the pipeline for women in science, since as Giuseppi points out, women faculty are important for attracting women graduate students.

Different types of institutions emphasize different aspects of education as reflected in their Carnegie Code Classifications. Formerly classified as Research I institutions, the new Carnegie Code Classification now refers to doctoral/research institutions–extensive, which award at least 50 doctoral degrees per year across 15 disciplines plus a wide range of baccalaureate programs. These institutions, along with doctoral/research institutions–intensive, which award at least 10 doctoral degrees per year across 3 or more disciplines, emphasize research productivity for tenure-track faculty for success in promotion and tenure. Good teaching is valued, but research serves as the lifeblood of the institution. In contrast, because of their mission, baccalaureate college–liberal arts institutions count undergraduate teaching more heavily in promotion and tenure, while expecting more modest research productivity. Despite these differing expectations, extreme time pressures and commitments to the institution become the similarity faced by faculty in both the doctoral/research institutions and the small liberal arts colleges.

These pressures and commitments explain the very similar responses to the e-mail questionnaire given by the POWRE awardees who come predominantly from public doctoral/research institutions to those of the Clare Boothe Luce awardees, predominately at private and bacca-laureate colleges, who responded to this questionnaire. It also reveals the fallacy that small liberal arts colleges provide the panacea for balancing career and family. Although a teaching schedule may more easily be worked around a family schedule than some research agendas that require long hours in the laboratory or months in the field, the heavy teaching schedule often results in less than adequate research time and productivity, particularly as the faculty member becomes more senior and further from graduate training. The absence of graduate students, postdocs, and technicians may retard gathering of research data, ultimately making grant applications and renewals more difficult for faculty at small liberal arts colleges. Without grants, it is usually impossible for faculty in the sciences to do their research, unlike their colleagues in the humanities or some areas of the social sciences. This may become exacerbated for women, in particular, over time because they have less access to networks than do their male colleagues. Eminent women scientists for example, report that exclusion from information-rich "old boy" networks constituted critical impediments to their success. This exclusion was compounded by the lack of senior women to serve as role models to "counteract persistent negative images" in the workplace (Wasserman, 1998).

# Chapter 6

## A Brighter Future:
## Change the Institutions,
## Not the Women

How can we solve this dilemma faced by academic women scientists and engineers? The 450 women I surveyed are highly educated and successful. They have completed Ph.D. degrees and postdoctoral experiences at the most prestigious institutions in the country. They have succeeded in obtaining a coveted tenure-track position at either a Research I institution or a highly ranked small liberal arts college. Each has competed to obtain a prestigious NSF or CBL award. Most still love their chosen field of science or engineering.

Yet they express frustration with problems, and in some cases, almost insurmountable barriers erected by institutional and foundational policies and procedures. From the interviews and responses to the e-mail questionnaires, we know that some disciplines, institutions, or individual timing of life events are better or worse than others. Encouraging mentors and role models, both male and female, do make a difference. A supportive spouse/partner is critical. But the bottom line remains the same: Most of these women struggle to have both a life and a career as a scientist or engineer.

The United States cannot afford to lose these highly trained, well-placed women scientists and engineers from its workforce. The increased reliance of the global economy on science and technology, coupled with the limitations placed on the use of immigration to fill science and technology workforce shortages in the wake of September 11 in the United States, underlines how critical enabling these women to flourish as scientists and engineers has become. What can leaders in academia, foundations, and scientific professional societies do to nourish these women? What policies and practices help, and what institutional barriers need to be removed or changed?

Just as women at very different institutions gave similar responses to the e-mail questions, women in different disciplines that have widely varying percentages of women do not give disparate discipline-based responses to the e-mail questions. Although engineering only has 6% women faculty, while biology has 28% and the social sciences have 28% (see Table 2, Chapter 4), women biologists, engineers, and social scientists have remarkably similar responses to the questionnaire. This suggests that the problem is apparently the institutional structure that operates in sociology as well as engineering.

How can these problems expressed by women scientists and engineers from different subdisciplines who work in all types of institutions be solved? What approaches are more helpful? Which are less helpful?

### Approaches for Funding Agencies

One level at which these questions can be asked and answered is what works and doesn't work especially well about the POWRE and CBL programs? This information should be useful not only to the foundations funding these particular programs that attempt to facilitate the careers of women scientists and engineers. It should also provide insight to institutions attempting to craft and implement policies to attract and retain women in these fields.

As Table 19 shows, the POWRE awardees gave more than a dozen different responses each year to the question: What do you like least/find most problematic about POWRE? The methodology used for categorizing these responses was the same one followed for categorization

**TABLE 19** Total Responses to Question 3

Question 3: What do you like least/find most problematic about POWRE?

| CATEGORIES | 1997 % OF RESPONSES | | 1998 % OF RESPONSES | | 1999 % OF RESPONSES | | 2000 % OF RESPONSES | |
|---|---|---|---|---|---|---|---|---|
| 1 Fund limit | 31.3 | (21/67) | 20.2 | (24/119) | 20.4 | (20/98) | 15.2 | (16/105) |
| 2 Perception as less prestigious/competitive | 7.5 | (5/67) | 9.2 | (22/119) | 15.1 | (18/98) | 18.5 | (20/105) |
| 3 Fact that it is for women only | 19.4 | (13/67) | 16.8 | (20/119) | 10.1 | (10/98) | 10.2 | (11/105) |
| 4 No problems | 17.9 | (12/67) | 16.8 | (20/119) | 24.5 | (24/98) | 17.6 | (19/105) |
| 5 Time limit | 16.4 | (11/67) | 27.7 | (33/119) | 21.4 | (21/98) | 31.5 | (34/105) |
| 6 Lack of available information | 7.5 | (5/67) | 3.4 | (4/119) | 2.0 | (2/98) | 4.6 | (5/105) |
| 7 Requires research away from home institution | 6.0 | (4/67) | 4.2 | (5/119) | 1.0 | (1/98) | 2.8 | (3/105) |
| 8 Review process | 3.0 | (2/67) | 7.6 | (9/119) | 6.1 | (6/98) | 3.7 | (4/105) |
| 9 No answer | 1.5 | (1/67) | 3.4 | (4/119) | 2.0 | (2/98) | 0 | (0/105) |
| 10 Administrative/bureaucratic hold-ups | 1.5 | (4/67) | 1.7 | (2/119) | 3.1 | (3/98) | 3.7 | (4/105) |
| 11 Need ability to conduct research abroad | 1.5 | (1/67) | — | (0/119) | 0 | (0/98) | — | (0/105) |
| 12 Fosters competition among women in departments | 1.5 | (1/67) | 1.7 | (2/119) | 3.1 | (3/98) | — | (0/105) |
| 13 Doesn't facilitate networking/only benefits recipients | 1.5 | (1/67) | <1 | (1/119) | 3.1 | (3/98) | 4.6 | (5/105) |
| 14 Discontinued | — | | — | | 3.1 | (3/98) | 5.5 | (6/105) |
| 15 Supplemental grants removed | — | | — | | — | | <1 | (1/105) |
| 16 Don't like the name | — | | — | | — | | <1 | (1/105) |

of the other data published from this POWRE study (Rosser & Ziese-niss, 2000). The categories emerged from the coding of the textual replies. The three categories in Table 18 represent groupings of more similar responses that emerged from a discussion of the categories and data at a national conference by 30 social scientists, scientists, and engineers whose work focuses on women and science (Rosser, 1999).

Table 20 groups the responses to question 3 under three broad categories: gender related; content or parameters of POWRE itself; NSF administration of the program. Gender related includes responses where awardees indicated that targeting POWRE for women only was especially positive or negative. These are some of the responses from the awardees that illustrate the parameters of the category.

> The biggest problem with POWRE is that it essentially requires (or favors) that research be done away from your home base at another university or research lab. In my own case, I had to leave my daughter and husband at home, which would be the case for most all academic women with working spouses and families. Although the research opportunity is wonderful, the additional personal (and familial) sacrifice of being away from home is hardly worth the professional gain to me. (1997 respondent 1)
>
> My male colleagues do not value the POWRE award as highly as other NSF awards. They assume that because the target recipients are women, that the awards are not as competitive as other NSF programs. I wouldn't say this is a problem with POWRE, but if there are some male scientists who have elected to take time off to raise families, or who are entering academic positions after a long time away the same difficulties apply and there should be a POWRE-like opportunity for them. (1997 respondent 9)
>
> POWRE has helped me on two occasions and both times it was an enormous boon to my career, first by allowing me to purchase a critical piece of equipment and most recently by making my yearlong sabbatical possible. The thing that I like least about the program is being labeled by it. That is, many people have significantly less respect for monies I have obtained through POWRE despite the good it did for me. (2000 respondent 23)

**TABLE 20** Categorization of Question 3 (revised to include "doesn't facilitate networking/only benefits recipients")

## Question 3: What do you like least/find most problematic about POWRE?

| CATEGORIES | RESPONSE NUMBERS[a] | 1997 | 1998 | MEANS OF RESPONSES (%) 1999 | 2000 |
|---|---|---|---|---|---|
| A Gender related | 2, 3, 7, 12 | 8.6 | 8.0 | 7.3 | 7.9 |
| B Content or parameters of POWRE itself | 1, 5, 11, 13 | 12.7 | 12.2 | 11.2 | 12.8 |
| C NSF administration of the program | 6, 8, 10 | 4.0 | 4.2 | 3.7 | 4.0 |

[a] "No answer" responses were not included in the calculations in these tables, since it was unclear whether they should be included in Category B or C. Responses 4, 14, 15, and 16 were not included in the calculations of the means here because these responses were not present for all years. Note that even when the data were recalculated, with "no problems" added to B or C, the relative position of the categories remained constant.

My single concern about the POWRE grant is that it is a "women only" grant, and that this may be perceived as less competitive than other NSF programs. My hope is that the grant recipients will perform excellent research and produce high-quality results, thus defining POWRE as a highly competitive program. (1997 respondent 25)

To me, the program statement had an "old-fashioned" feel. I felt a little funny applying for the money, as though I had to argue that I was disadvantaged and therefore less than competent in order to successfully compete for the funds. It would have felt better somehow to argue that I have great ideas and deserve funding. (2000 respondent 49)

In writing the project summary or the proposal in such a way as to explain how the project qualifies under the rules for POWRE, one writes a document, which when viewed by male colleagues invites their scorn. The structure of the proposal should be changed so that one writes a professional proposal which one would not mind having one's male colleagues read, and then an auxiliary two-page statement explaining why the applicant thinks that she qualifies for the program. (1997 respondent 49) (Note that in later years, the program was changed to structure proposal submission in this way.)

The problem that I faced with POWRE, in the first call for proposals, was that I competed against a more junior member of my department. Although we were in very different categories, I felt that she was disadvantaged in the competition by my application (and probably vice versa). In the previous structure of the programs, we would not have been in competition. I guess my point is that unlike categories funded under a single program (initial research vs. visiting professorships for instance), this perhaps stacks the deck against some younger (start-up type) candidates, who may have less perspective on why they are at such a vulnerable point in their careers. They also potentially disadvantage applicants in departments who may have several women on staff, which seems like something NSF might want to encourage systemically. (1997 respondent 44)

The greatest dissatisfaction, almost double that for category A and almost quadruple that for category C, centered on the content or parameters of POWRE itself. This category referred to conditions such as limits placed on time, funds, and site of research imposed in the program solicitation by NSF. Quotations from awardees suggest their frustration with the POWRE parameters, although a substantial percentage (17–24%) of respondents all 4 years found "no problems" with POWRE.

> The upper limit of funding given for a POWRE grant was $50,000. In my case, this was not really sufficient to fund my project costs (about $75,000), and much less than what I would have asked for in a standard NSF application to the SBE division. (Indirect costs absorb 50% of grant funds these days leaving little actual funding for the researcher.) The result was that, in order to conduct my research and accept the grant, I had to ask my own university to absorb many of my costs. They ended up doing so but now, instead of feeling as if my scholarly standing increased as a result of the grant, I feel as if I owe the administration a favor. I believe that an increased limit on POWRE grants, at least a funding level that more favorably compares to other NSF programs, will avoid creating a "second-class" image of POWRE grants. (1997 respondent 15)

> Grant size should be larger and the period longer so that you can get more research going. (2000 respondent 25)

> Unlike standard NSF grants which often provide funding for 2–3 years, POWRE funding is capped (in $ amount) and typically provides funding for a single year. While I understand that there are budgetary constraints, allowing a larger amount of funding for multiple years will allow POWRE researchers to make more substantive long-term proposals. (1997 respondent 32)

> The seed-grant is only for 1 year — 2 years would be ideal to make a significant impact on the new field of research the person is embarking on. (1999 respondent 1)

> I would like to have had more freedom putting together a stay at a foreign laboratory since most of the work in my field is being conducted in France, Israel, and Switzerland. (1997 respondent 9)

Awardees expressed only minor dissatisfactions with NSF administration processes of review, bureaucracy, and information surrounding POWRE.

Most problematic: finding who on NSF staff to talk to about proposal development. Since it is interdisciplinary, I was passed around to several people to talk to. But since it was such a new program, answers were always unclear and fuzzy. (1997 respondent 10)

If POWRE does not allow one to put in for REU [Research Experience for Undergraduate] student help, I will find this problematic. I am unclear on the details and plan to inquire to my program director. My POWRE grant is predominately salary for myself. I could not squeeze into the grant a salary for student assistance and was relying on REU to help me with that. (2000 respondent 50)

I don't know very much about the review process, but my understanding is that the proposals were not sent for outside review, and that the panel was very broad and interdisciplinary. This bothered me for two reasons. First, I had written the proposal with the Linguistics Panel in mind. Second, what guarantees that the appropriate expertise will be represented on the interdisciplinary panel? (1997 respondent 2)

Table 21 shows the responses to question 3 when the data from all 4 years are pooled and the responses are categorized by the NSF directorate of the awardee; this categorization assumes that the NSF directorate granting the POWRE award serves as an indicator of the discipline or field of the awardee. (Note that for data interpretation, education and human resources is removed since the numbers are smaller and all awardees come from disciplinary backgrounds included in other NSF directorates.)

The similarities of responses among the different directorates and across years emerge as the most striking overall finding. The top five categories, with the possible exception of perception as less prestigious/competitive (response 2) because of responses from awardees from the directorates of social, behavioral, and economic (SBE) sciences and mathematics and physical sciences (MPS), uniformly represent the highest percentage of responses across all directorates. The frustration with supporting research of individual investigators as a way to solve the problem is recognized by some awardees who note the importance of institutional approaches.

**TABLE 21** Responses to Question 3 According to Directorate

Question 3: What do you like least/find most problematic about POWRE?

| CATEGORIES | SBE % OF | SBE RESPONSES | MPS % OF | MPS RESPONSES | ENG % OF | ENG RESPONSES | EHR[a] % OF | EHR RESPONSES | CISE % OF | CISE RESPONSES | BIO % OF | BIO RESPONSES | GEO % OF | GEO RESPONSES |
|---|---|---|---|---|---|---|---|---|---|---|---|---|---|---|
| 1 Fund limit | 23.8 | (15/63) | 15.5 | (13/84) | 15.9 | (11/69) | 16.7 | (2/12) | 14.3 | (5/35) | 27.1 | (23/85) | 28.9 | (11/38) |
| 2 Perception as less prestigious/competitive | 7.9 | (5/63) | 7.1 | (6/84) | 15.9 | (11/69) | 0 | (0/12) | 14.3 | (5/35) | 14.1 | (12/85) | 13.2 | (5/38) |
| 3 Fact that it is for women only | 12.7 | (8/63) | 10.7 | (9/84) | 17.4 | (12/69) | 16.7 | (2/12) | 17.1 | (6/35) | 12.9 | (11/85) | 15.8 | (6/38) |
| 4 No problems | 23.8 | (15/63) | 26.2 | (22/84) | 11.6 | (8/69) | 41.7 | (5/12) | 20 | (7/35) | 22.9 | (11/85) | 13.2 | (5/38) |
| 5 Time limit | 27.0 | (17/63) | 16.7 | (14/84) | 34.8 | (24/69) | 16.7 | (2/12) | 20 | (7/35) | 37.6 | (32/85) | 15.8 | (6/38) |
| 6 Lack of available information | 1.6 | (1/63) | 2.4 | (2/84) | 5.8 | (4/69) | 8.3 | (1/12) | 5.7 | (2/35) | 5.9 | (5/85) | 2.6 | (1/38) |
| 7 Requires research away from home institution | 1.6 | (1/63) | 7.1 | (6/84) | 4.3 | (3/69) | 0 | (0/12) | 2.9 | (1/35) | 0 | (0/85) | 2.6 | (1/38) |
| 8 Review process | 7.9 | (5/63) | 8.3 | (7/84) | 4.3 | (3/69) | 16.7 | (2/12) | 2.9 | (1/35) | 2.4 | (2/85) | 2.6 | (1/38) |
| 9 No answer | 4.8 | (3/63) | 1.2 | (1/84) | 1.4 | (1/69) | 0 | (0/12) | 2.9 | (1/35) | 1.2 | (1/85) | 0 | (0/38) |
| 10 Administrative/bureaucratic hold-ups | 4.8 | (3/63) | 3.6 | (3/84) | 2.9 | (2/69) | 0 | (0/12) | 5.7 | (2/35) | 2.4 | (2/85) | 2.6 | (1/38) |
| 11 Need ability to conduct research abroad | 0 | (0/63) | 0 | (0/84) | 1.4 | (1/69) | 0 | (0/12) | 0 | (0/35) | 0 | (0/85) | 0 | (0/38) |
| 12 Fosters competition among women in departments | 1.6 | (1/63) | 1.2 | (1/84) | 0 | (0/69) | 0 | (0/12) | 0 | (0/35) | 2.4 | (2/85) | 5.3 | (2/38) |
| 13 Doesn't facilitate networking/only benefits recipients | 0 | (0/63) | 0 | (0/84) | 5.8 | (4/69) | 0 | (0/12) | 8.6 | (3/35) | 2.4 | (2/85) | 2.6 | (1/38) |
| 14 Discontinued | 3.2 | (2/63) | 3.6 | (3/84) | 0 | (0/69) | 0 | (0/12) | 2.9 | (1/35) | 1.2 | (1/85) | 5.3 | (2/38) |
| 15 Supplemental grants removed | 0 | (0/63) | 0 | (0/84) | 1.4 | (1/69) | 0 | (0/12) | 0 | (0/35) | 0 | (0/85) | 0 | (0/38) |
| 16 Don't like the name | 0 | (0/63) | 0 | (0/84) | 0 | (0/69) | 0 | (0/12) | 0 | (0/35) | 0 | (0/85) | 0 | (0/38) |

BIO = biological sciences; CISE = computer and information science and engineering; EHR = education and human resources; ENG = engineering; GEO = geosciences; MPS = mathematical and physical sciences; SBE = social, behavioral, and economic sciences

[a]Because of the low numbers of awardees, the EHR directorate should be carefully interpreted here. Many of the women representing this directorate have other disciplinary training and could be classified in other directorates. The EHR responses are not interpreted as a result.

I'm not sure how much sense it makes to try to foster women's participation in science and engineering through project-oriented programs. Probably, the lives of a few individual women (i.e., the grant recipients) will be made somewhat easier but it's hard to see how this significantly benefits women in the S&E professions in general. The development of networks among women scientists and engineers and programs to increase the visibility of women scientists and engineers within the S&E profession (such as the Research Professorship for Women program) would probably be of more general benefit than project-oriented awards. As far as I am aware, the POWRE program does not incorporate even the simplest attempt at networking, such as circulating a list of POWRE awardees. In addition, the limiting of project-oriented awards to any subgroup tends to carry the "second-class" taint. (1998 respondent 58)

In contrast to the POWRE awardees, the Clare Boothe Luce professors gave very different responses, both in terms of content and frequency to question 3. "What do you like least/find most problematic about the CBL Professorship?" As Table 22 shows, the overwhelming response (37%) of CBL professors was a "no problems" (response 4). Since the CBL program officer included this e-mail questionnaire in the required annual report, this may have affected this response, elevating the positive outcome. Need ability to conduct research abroad (response 11) became the most frequently cited problem (22%), with administrative/bureaucratic hold-ups (response 10) and doesn't facilitate networking/only benefits recipients (response 13) both mentioned by 12% of respondents.

Three new responses (17, 18, 19) not cited by the POWRE awardees, emerged from the CBL e-mail replies. Because of the relatively low number of CBL professors, compared to POWRE awardess, analyzing the CBL data for question 3 as done in Tables 20 and 21 for POWRE data, was not possible.

The quotations from the CBL professors themselves best describe problems with the award. Several CBL faculty found the prohibition on using funds for travel outside the United States to be problematic.

**TABLE 22** Total Responses to Question 3

Question 3: What do you like least/find most problematic about POWRE/CBL awards?

| CATEGORIES | 1997 | | 1998 | | 1999 | | 2000 | | CURRENT CBL PROFS. | |
|---|---|---|---|---|---|---|---|---|---|---|
| | % OF RESPONSES | RESPONSES | % OF RESPONSES | RESPONSES | % OF RESPONSES | RESPONSES | % OF RESPONSES | RESPONSES | % OF RESPONSES | |
| 1 Fund limit | 31.3 | (21/67) | 20.2 | (24/119) | 20.4 | (20/98) | 15.2 | (16/105) | — | — |
| 2 Perception as less prestigious/competitive | 7.5 | (5/67) | 9.2 | (22/119) | 15.1 | (18/98) | 18.5 | (20/105) | 7.3 | (3/41) |
| 3 Fact that it is for women only | 19.4 | (13/67) | 16.8 | (20/119) | 10.1 | (10/98) | 10.2 | (11/105) | — | — |
| 4 No problems | 17.9 | (12/67) | 16.8 | (20/119) | 24.5 | (24/98) | 17.6 | (19/105) | 36.6 | (15/41) |
| 5 Time limit | 16.4 | (11/67) | 27.7 | (33/119) | 21.4 | (21/98) | 31.5 | (34/105) | 4.9 | (2/41) |
| 6 Lack of available information | 7.5 | (5/67) | 3.4 | (4/119) | 2.0 | (2/98) | 4.6 | (5/105) | — | — |
| 7 Requires research away from home institution | 6.0 | (4/67) | 4.2 | (5/119) | 1.0 | (1/98) | 2.8 | (3/105) | — | — |
| 8 Review process | 3.0 | (2/67) | 7.6 | (9/119) | 6.1 | (6/98) | 3.7 | (4/105) | — | — |
| 9 No answer | 1.5 | (1/67) | 3.4 | (4/119) | 2.0 | (2/98) | — | (0/105) | 7.3 | (3/41) |
| 10 Administrative/bureaucratic hold-ups | 1.5 | (4/67) | 1.7 | (2/119) | 3.1 | (3/98) | 3.7 | (4/105). | 12.2 | (5/41) |
| 11 Need ability to conduct research abroad | 1.5 | (1/67) | — | (0/119) | 0 | (0/98) | — | (0/105) | 22 | (9/41) |
| 12 Fosters competition among women in departments | 1.5 | (1/67) | 1.7 | (2/119) | 3.1 | (3/98) | — | (0/105) | — | — |
| 13 Doesn't facilitate networking/only benefits recipients | 1.5 | (1/67) | <1 | (1/119) | 3.1 | (3/98) | 4.6 | (5/105) | 12.2 | (5/41) |
| 14 Discontinued | — | — | — | — | 3.1 | (3/98) | 5.5 | (6/105) | — | — |
| 15 Supplemental grants removed | — | — | — | — | — | — | <1 | (1/105) | — | — |
| 16 Doesn't like the name | — | — | — | — | — | — | <1 | (1/105) | — | — |
| 17 Can't use CBL to support technical staff | | | | | | | | | 4.9 | (2/41) |
| 18 Doesn't like conferences | | | | | | | | | 2.4 | (1/41) |
| 19 Institution relies on CBL money for supplies | | | | | | | | | 2.4 | (1/41) |

Funds cannot be used to support international travel and research! Professorship lasts only 5 years and is nonrenewable. (respondent 39)

Restriction to domestic travel — many important conferences in my field are held in Canada or overseas. (respondent 37)

The only small glitch that I've run up against so far is not being able to use the sabbatical funding (which is WONDERFUL — thanks!!!) to pursue scholarly activities at institutions outside of the USA. Science is such an international effort nowadays that it seems an odd restriction. (respondent 23)

It would be nice if travel to conferences outside the U.S. could be funded. (respondent 21)

Given that the departments and institutions may use the CBL funds to defray costs that they must pay for non-CBL faculty, the restriction preventing funding international travel might be one way to prevent institutions from excessive overreliance on CBL funds, which some faculty cite as a problem.

The most problematic aspect of the CBL Professorship is the tendency for me and the department to rely on that funding to pay for my standard supplies, equipment, and conference costs. (respondent 11)

Many mentioned a desire to interact more with other CBL professors.

Lack of interaction with other CBL Professors. (respondent 14)

There is nothing really "problematic." It would be nice to meet more often with other CBL professors. (respondent 15)

I would like a way to meet informally with other "past" CBL professors (both from XXX and maybe from other area colleges where we could get a new perspective). This kind of informal mentoring can be especially beneficial early in your career when you are making so many new decisions based on so little prior knowledge. (respondent 6)

The responses to question 4: What do you like best/find most useful about POWRE? (Table 23) provide not only the mirror image responses to question 3, but they also reveal considerable information about the strengths of POWRE. Table 24 shows relatively the same rankings of low to high for the three categories as expressed for question 3. Gender-related responses were positive and reflected opposite opinions from those who felt uncomfortable that POWRE was for women only. Despite the negative-to-ambivalent feelings expressed in response to question 3 about POWRE being less prestigious and for women only, many respondents to question 4 liked the fact that POWRE helps women who have had career interruptions (response 6).

> The POWRE program is designated for women who have exceptional challenges that most people in academia do not have any feel for. (1997 respondent 57)
>
> POWRE is a great and unconventional funding source for scientists who come from unconventional circumstances. While many successful women scientists, like myself, don't feel that they have been individually disadvantaged for being female, they are still more likely to be the one trying to keep all the balls in the air for a family with small children while meeting the travel and time commitment requirements for doing science and professional service. POWRE implicitly recognizes that and provides an alternative award system. (1997 respondent 44)
>
> It provided me an opportunity to support a graduate student and an undergraduate student in the laboratory! That has been a great help!!! It has been difficult getting funding at this stage after being out of the research area for a while but the POWRE provided me the chance to pursue the research area again. (2000 respondent 36)
>
> Well, I guess I got one because I was a hard luck case and getting a POWRE award is going to make me once again very competitive. I was totally disabled for a few years and then gradually came back. The POWRE award is giving the resources I need in this transition period. I know it is already helping, and I am very appreciative of having received this award. (1977 respondent 47)

In contrast, the positive response to the content or parameters of POWRE itself reflected in response to question 4 was lower than the negative response reflected in Table 23 in response to question 3. This may suggest that NSF's decision to terminate POWRE, and have ADVANCE succeed it, reflected an appropriate response to negative reactions to the content or parameters of POWRE itself. Many

TABLE 23  Total Responses to Question 4

## Question 4: What do you like best/find most useful about POWRE?

| | CATEGORIES | 1997 % OF RESPONSES | | 1998 % OF RESPONSES | | 1999 % OF RESPONSES | | 2000 % OF RESPONSES | |
|---|---|---|---|---|---|---|---|---|---|
| 1 | Opens door for advancement/research opportunities | 26.9 | (18/67) | 46.2 | (55/119) | 21.4 | (21/98) | 30.5 | (32/105) |
| 2 | Flexibility of funds allows for "nontraditional" research | 20.9 | (14/67) | 10.9 | (13/119) | 28.6 | (28/98) | 20.4 | (22/105) |
| 3 | Getting funding for various needs | 8.9 | (6/67) | 5.0 | (6/119) | 8.2 | (8/98) | 11.1 | (12/105) |
| 4 | Quick response time | 7.5 | (5/67) | 4.2 | (5/119) | 1.0 | (1/98) | 0 | (0/105) |
| 5 | Foot in the door for other funding | 11.9 | (8/67) | 5.0 | (6/119) | 8.2 | (8/98) | 9.3 | (10/105) |
| 6 | Helps women who have had career interruptions | 16.4 | (11/67) | 8.4 | (10/119) | 26.5 | (26/98) | 12.0 | (13/105) |
| 7 | Panel review format | 1.5 | (1/67) | 1.7 | (2/119) | 0 | (0/98) | <1 | (1/105) |
| 8 | Simplicity of application process | 3.0 | (2/67) | 0 | (0/119) | 2.0 | (2/98) | 1.9 | (2/105) |
| 9 | Allows for combination of teaching and research | 4.5 | (3/67) | 1.7 | (2/119) | 5.1 | (5/98) | 4.6 | (5/105) |
| 10 | Allows for relocation/visiting professorship | 3.0 | (2/67) | 8.4 | (10/119) | 5.1 | (5/98) | 8.3 | (9/105) |
| 11 | Being able to compete in a restricted pool (i.e., women only) | 6.0 | (4/67) | 5.0 | (6/119) | 1.0 | (1/98) | 5.6 | (6/105) |
| 12 | No answer | 1.5 | (1/67) | 1.7 | (2/119) | 1.0 | (1/98) | <1 | (1/105) |
| 13 | Acknowledges exceptional challenges of women | 3.0 | (2/67) | 9.2 | (11/119) | 5.1 | (5/98) | 10.5 | (11/105) |

**TABLE 24** Categorization of Question 4

## Question 4: What do you like best/find most useful about POWRE?

| CATEGORIES | RESPONSE NUMBERS[a] | MEANS OF RESPONSES (%) | | | |
|---|---|---|---|---|---|
| | | 1997 | 1998 | 1999 | 2000 |
| A Gender related | 6, 11, 13 | 8.5 | 7.5 | 10.9 | 9.4 |
| B Content or parameters of POWRE itself | 1, 2, 3, 5, 9, 10 | 12.7 | 12.9 | 12.8 | 14.0 |
| C NSF administration of the program | 4, 7, 8 | 4.0 | 2.0 | 1.0 | < 1.0 |

[a] "No answer" responses (response 12) were not included in the calculation of the means in this table.

respondents indicated an appreciation because POWRE opens the door for advancement/research opportunities (response 1), especially for difficult-to-fund nontraditional research (response 2). Grouping responses 1 and 2 with getting funding for various needs (response 3) and foot in the door for other funding (response 5) illustrates the pressure POWRE awardees feel to obtain funding to support their research in these times of tight resource constraints.

Allows me to take on a pilot project dear to my heart which might not otherwise be funded. (1997 respondent 46)

I love the research and teaching program I've been able to establish thanks to the POWRE program. Once I had received government funding (this is the only program I was eligible for as a nontenure track faculty member), I was able to get industrial donations to set up a lab for 3–4 grad students and 1 undergrad to do cutting-edge research. (1999 respondent 21)

I think the visiting professor program has great potential for all sides. Also it is nice for people to have a way to get back in when their career is interrupted, as it more often is for women (I guess one could open that part to men as well). The subtle barriers don't go away easily. The visiting professor program especially can help people discover what some of those might be for an institution. (1997 respondent 64)

The most useful aspect of POWRE has been the way the grant has allowed me to reduce my regular teaching commitments to free up the time I needed to acquire additional training that I would otherwise never have been able to do. (2000 respondent 19)

I got funding that will be very helpful to me in setting up a lab and trying to do research that will get me tenure. What more can I say? (1997 respondent 41)

The funding can be used for my own salary, not just students or postdocs. (2000 respondent 37)

The NSF administration of the program registered the lowest response; this may reflect a smoothly running bureaucracy, since when programs are administered well, the administration appears relatively invisible.

The simplicity of the application process; it was more straightforward and clear than many NSF grant programs. (1997 respondent 31)

The rapid (!) decision time is great! I also think it's great that the funding is available for women at critical points in their careers. In my case, the POWRE grant may well play a pivotal role in my tenure case. (1998 respondent 14)

Receiving a grant — having money for research!! I also think using the panel review format is very good for this program. (1997 respondent 10)

Table 25 shows the responses to question 4 when the data from all 4 years are pooled and the responses are categorized by the NSF directorate of the awardee; this categorization assumes that the NSF directorate granting the POWRE award serves as an indicator of the discipline or field of the awardee. (Note that for data interpretation, education and human resources is removed since the numbers are smaller and all awardees come from disciplinary backgrounds included in other NSF directorates.)

As was the case with Table 21, which illustrated the directorate responses to question 3, Table 25 reveals the similarities of response among the different directorates and across all 4 years.

As suggested in the previous chapter and by their responses to question 3, the CBL professors found many positive aspects to the award. As Table 26 documents, the CBL professors overwhelmingly (46%) found "getting funding for various needs" (response 3) to be what they like best/found most useful.

The CBL Professorship has given me the freedom to extend my junior leave from the typical half year to a full year by providing salary support for an additional semester. This time will be invaluable as I finish up projects begun by undergraduates in my laboratory, write, and begin the projects outlined in my recently funded NIH grant. (respondent 41)

The professional expense account has allowed me to pursue some research avenues that are not funded by my NIH grant. This has opened new doors for my research group which have been quite successful. In addition, I think that having the professorship helped me to get grants at the start of my independent career. (respondent 30)

**TABLE 25** Responses to Question 4 According to Directorate

## Question 4: What do you like best/find most useful about POWRE?

| CATEGORIES | SBE % OF | RESPONSES | MPS % OF | RESPONSES | ENG % OF | RESPONSES | EHR[a] % OF | RESPONSES | CISE % OF | RESPONSES | BIO % OF | RESPONSES | GEO % OF | RESPONSES |
|---|---|---|---|---|---|---|---|---|---|---|---|---|---|---|
| 1 Opens door for advancement/research opportunities | 31.7 | (20/63) | 29.8 | (25/84) | 30.4 | (21/69) | 25 | (3/12) | 31.4 | (11/35) | 34.1 | (29/85) | 42.1 | (16/38) |
| 2 Flexibility of funds allows for "non-traditional" research | 22.2 | (14/63) | 17.9 | (15/84) | 17.4 | (12/69) | 58.3 | (7/12) | 11.4 | (4/35) | 18.8 | (16/85) | 21.1 | (8/38) |
| 3 Getting funding for various needs | 9.5 | (6/63) | 7.1 | (6/84) | 4.3 | (3/69) | 16.7 | (2/12) | 5.7 | (2/35) | 10.6 | (9/85) | 10.5 | (4/38) |
| 4 Quick response time | 4.8 | (3/63) | 2.4 | (2/84) | 1.4 | (1/69) | 0 | (0/12) | 2.9 | (1/35) | 3.5 | (3/85) | 2.6 | (1/38) |
| 5 Foot in the door for other funding | 12.7 | (8/63) | 4.8 | (4/84) | 7.2 | (5/69) | 8.3 | (1/12) | 4.3 | (5/35) | 8.2 | (7/85) | 5.3 | (2/38) |
| 6 Helps women who have had career interruptions | 9.5 | (6/63) | 11.3 | (12/84) | 15.9 | (11/69) | 8.3 | (1/12) | 20.0 | (7/35) | 18.8 | (16/85) | 13.2 | (5/38) |
| 7 Panel review format | 4.8 | (3/63) | 1.2 | (1/84) | 0 | (0/69) | 0 | (0/12) | 0 | (0/35) | 0 | (0/85) | 0 | (0/38) |
| 8 Simplicity of application process | 0 | (0/63) | 0 | (0/84) | 2.9 | (2/69) | 0 | (0/12) | 5.7 | (2/35) | 2.4 | (2/85) | 0 | (0/38) |
| 9 Allows for combination of teaching and research | 3.2 | (2/63) | 6.0 | (5/84) | 7.2 | (5/69) | 0 | (0/12) | 0 | (0/35) | 2.4 | (2/85) | 2.6 | (1/38) |
| 10 Allows for relocation/visiting professorship | 3.2 | (2/63) | 16.7 | (14/84) | 5.8 | (4/69) | 0 | (0/12) | 8.6 | (3/35) | 4.7 | (4/85) | 2.6 | (1/38) |
| 11 Being able to compete in a restricted pool (i.e., women only) | 3.2 | (2/63) | 3.6 | (3/84) | 5.8 | (4/69) | 8.3 | (1/12) | 2.9 | (1/35) | 3.5 | (3/85) | 5.3 | (2/38) |
| 12 No answer | 1.6 | (1/63) | 1.2 | (1/84) | 1.4 | (1/69) | 0 | (0/12) | 0 | (0/35) | 0 | (0/85) | 2.6 | (1/38) |
| 13 Acknowledges exceptional challenges of women | 6.3 | (4/63) | 6.0 | (5/84) | 8.7 | (6/69) | 0 | (0/12) | 8.6 | (3/35) | 10.6 | (9/85) | 2.6 | (1/38) |

[a]Because of the low numbers of awardees, the EHR directorate should be carefully interpreted here. Many of the women representing this directorate have other disciplinary training and could be classified in other directorates. We have chosen not to analyze the EHR responses.

BIO = biological sciences; CISE = computer and information science and engineering; EHR = education and human resources; ENG = engineering; GEO = geosciences; MPS = mathematical and physical sciences; SBE = social, behavioral, and economic sciences.

**TABLE 26** Total Responses to Question 4

Question 4: What do you like best/find most useful about POWRE/CBL awards?

| | CATEGORIES | 1997 % OF RESPONSES | | 1998 % OF RESPONSES | | 1999 % OF RESPONSES | | 2000 % OF RESPONSES | | CURRENT CBL PROFS. % OF RESPONSES | |
|---|---|---|---|---|---|---|---|---|---|---|---|
| 1 | Opens door for advancement/research opportunities | 26.9 | (18/67) | 46.2 | (55/119) | 21.4 | (21/98) | 30.5 | (32/105) | 2.4 | (1/41) |
| 2 | Flexibility of funds allows for "nontraditional" research | 20.9 | (14/67) | 10.9 | (13/119) | 28.6 | (28/98) | 20.4 | (22/105) | 12.2 | (5/41) |
| 3 | Getting funding for various needs | 8.9 | (6/67) | 5.0 | (6/119) | 8.2 | (8/98) | 11.1 | (12/105) | 46.3 | (19/41) |
| 4 | Quick response time | 7.5 | (5/67) | 4.2 | (5/119) | 1.0 | (1/98) | 0 | (0/105) | — | — |
| 5 | Foot in the door for other funding | 11.9 | (8/67) | 5.0 | (6/119) | 8.2 | (8/98) | 9.3 | (10/105) | 9.8 | (4/41) |
| 6 | Helps women who have had career interruptions | 16.4 | (11/67) | 8.4 | (10/119) | 26.5 | (26/98) | 12.0 | (13/105) | — | — |
| 7 | Panel review format | 1.5 | (1/67) | 1.7 | (2/119) | 0 | (0/98) | <1 | (1/105) | — | — |
| 8 | Simplicity of application process | 3.0 | (2/67) | 0 | (0/119) | 2.0 | (2/98) | 1.9 | (2/105) | — | — |
| 9 | Allows for combination of teaching and research | 4.5 | (3/67) | 1.7 | (2/119) | 5.1 | (5/98) | 4.6 | (5/105) | 2.4 | (1/41) |
| 10 | Allows for relocation/visiting professorship | 3.0 | (2/67) | 8.4 | (10/119) | 5.1 | (5/98) | 8.3 | (9/105) | — | — |
| 11 | Being able to compete in a restricted pool (i.e., women only) | 6.0 | (4/67) | 5.0 | (6/119) | 1.0 | (1/98) | 5.6 | (6/105) | — | — |
| 12 | No answer | 1.5 | (1/67) | 1.7 | (2/119) | 1.0 | (1/98) | <1 | (1/105) | 2.4 | (1/41) |
| 13 | Acknowledges exceptional challenges of women | 3.0 | (2/67) | 9.2 | (11/119) | 5.1 | (5/98) | 10.5 | (11/105) | 9.8 | (4/41) |
| 14 | Extend leave/sabbatical | | | | | | | | | 4.9 | (2/41) |
| 15 | Networking | | | | | | | | | 7.3 | (3/41) |
| 16 | Student-faculty collaboration | | | | | | | | | 17.1 | (7/41) |
| 17 | Child care | | | | | | | | | 2.4 | (1/41) |
| 18 | Distinguished | | | | | | | | | 12.2 | (5/41) |

Several (12%) noted the importance of the flexibility of funding (response 2), as the following quotations illustrate.

> Flexible source of funding for research support (equipment, supplies, etc.). Provides wonderful collaborative opportunity for student researchers and professor. (respondent 39)
>
> The most useful thing is the freedom to determine how to best spend the discretionary funds. I can use the funds to hire research assistants if needed without going through a lengthy proposal process. I can use the funds to buy myself some course release time so that I can spend more time on research and on mentoring female students. (respondent 36)
>
> Funding for research to use at my own discretion, for travel, books, child care, etc. (respondent 24)

Some CBL professors (10%) especially liked the award's acknowledgment of the exceptional challenges of women (response 13):

> The CBL Professorship is a very distinguished award, and I am honored to hold the title. In addition, I appreciate the vision of Ms. Luce and her desire to support female scientists. As a CBL professor I feel even more compelled to promote the advancement of women in the sciences. (respondent 32)

In contrast to the POWRE responses, as noted in the previous chapter, several (17%) also appreciated the student-faculty collaboration (response 16) encouraged by the CBL Professorship.

> The opportunity to be both teaching and researching with my students is one of the best parts of the CBL Professorship. I am looking forward to setting up my lab here at Rockhurst this summer to provide my students with experiences on state-of-the-art equipment tackling pertinent questions. This would not have been possible without the professorship. There is real potential to positively impact on my students. I hope to share with them my love of science and excitement about research to hopefully ignite in them a similar excitement. (respondent 20)

I like teaching and advising undergraduate women in a field of science that is still largely male-dominated. I find it very rewarding to encourage and mentor young women and look forward to seeing them go on to graduate school and beyond. If I have had any influence in encouraging these women to pursue environmental science careers, I will feel rewarded. (respondent 38)

Several (12%) underlined the distinction and prestige of the award; one succinctly summed it up, "I like the money and the fame."

## Systemic Approaches Through ADVANCE

Responses to questions 1 and 2, especially when coupled with the problems expressed in response to question 3 about the problems with the content or parameters of POWRE itself and the positive response to question 4 about the need to help women who have had career interruptions, suggest the need for support that extends beyond the research of individual women scientists and engineers. Many of the qualitative statements of POWRE awardees, from which the categories for the tables emerged, particularly underline the need for institutional, systemic approaches to balance career with family, deal with problems resulting from low numbers of women in some disciplines and the stereotyping they may encounter, as well as more overt discrimination and harassment. (Rosser & Lane, 2002; Rosser & Zieseniss, 2000).

When hearing the results of the first 2 years of awardee responses to the questionnaire in June 1998, NSF program officers reinforced the perception expressed by some awardees of a need for institutional approaches. The NSF program officers at the presentation requested that a question focused on institutional approaches be included in the e-mail questionnaire to the 1999 awardees. Responding to that request, the e-mail questionnaire sent to the 1999 awardees included the following question.

If the POWRE program is discontinued due to affirmative action concerns, do you think that an NSF program that takes an institutional approach would be a good idea? This would be a program to encourage institutional transformation regarding the culture of science and to increase gender and ethnic diversity among scientists for both faculty and students. Please briefly provide your views on this.

Several faculty expressed their opposition to institutional approaches, citing their doubts about the effectiveness of such approaches and their appreciation of awards to support the research of individual investigators.

> I suspect the "power" (if you will) of the POWRE program would be diluted by converting the program to an institutional approach, simply because I suspect fewer research dollars would go into the hands of fewer women scientists. Also, I would not be surprised if such a program raised as many flags as the current program seems to be raising (or such as I infer from the comment about affirmative action concerns). I would think such a program would be a red flag to republican policymakers in Congress. (1999 respondent 10)
>
> No, I have not ever seen these programs work effectively. (1999 respondent 18)
>
> I hope POWRE will not be discontinued. Regarding a program to encourage institutional transformation, no, I don't think this is a good idea. This seems to reward institutions that have not done a good job recruiting women faculty. I don't think the laboratory culture is a major problem, rather the perceived workload at research universities. Perhaps a better way would be to discriminate against departments that do not have a representative faculty. For example, departmental awards or multi-institutional awards (such as REUs, etc.) could have a statement regarding the faculty representation and this could be assessed by the reviewers. (1999 respondent 80)

On the whole, respondents, although grateful for their POWRE award, understood the importance of institutional approaches to alleviate barriers for women.

> I would agree that a broadened program that focused on the institution could be a very good idea. The biggest problem I have faced, together with friends and colleagues around the country, is the set of attitudes of department chairs and deans. They always seem to say the right things, but maintain the status quo through traditional means. While some young faculty are clearly favored by this system, there is evidence that they pay a high price for becoming part of it. I

don't know if there is anything NSF can do to intervene in this process. However, funding for organized research and teaching units that cut across departmental and college lines of authority could be extremely useful to women and minority faculty. These units seem to allow faculty with like interests to associate and create new organizational structures. Perhaps this is a way NSF could help to break the power of traditional hierarchies. (1999 respondent 17)

I think that increasing both gender and ethnic diversity in science at the student and faculty levels is something we should all be striving for. If NSF could come up with an institutional approach to this I think that would be a good idea. However, I have no idea, personally, how that could be done. Even institutions that have these goals have problems meeting them, partly because academic departments are involved. For instance, in the hiring process you get into lots of trouble if the administration tries to dictate who gets hired into specific departments. Incentives can be given but the final choice can't be the administration's or the person hired is at a disadvantage with their colleagues from the start. Perhaps I haven't fully understood how an institution would go about trying to transform the culture of science. (1999 respondent 9)

In fiscal year 2001, NSF launched the ADVANCE initiative to succeed POWRE.

ADVANCE has two categories to include institutional, rather than individual, solutions to empower women to participate fully in science and technology. The NSF encouraged institutional solutions, in addition to the individual solution permitted under the category of Fellows Awards, because of "increasing recognition that the lack of women's full participation at the senior level of academe is often a systemic consequence of academic culture" (NSF, 2001b, p. 2). Under ADVANCE, Institutional Transformation Awards, ranging up to $750,000 per year for up to 5 years, promote the increased participation and advancement of women; Leadership Awards recognize the work of outstanding organizations of individuals and enable them to sustain, intensify, and initiate new activity (NSF, 2001b).

In October 2001 the first 8 institutions receiving ADVANCE awards were announced (NSF, 2001c):

- The Georgia Institute of Technology is creating a network of termed professorships, institutionalizing a formal training process on tenure and promotion, gathering information on equity and advancement, holding leadership retreats, and strengthening family friendly practices.
- New Mexico State University intends to increase the number of women in its tenure-track positions in science, mathematics, and engineering by establishing a Committee on the Status of Women to monitor progress and identify ways in which university programs can be better targeted to support the advancement of women.
- The University of Washington is creating a Center for Institutional Change to design and implement programs to eliminate obstacles to women's full participation and advancing in the science, engineering, and mathematics fields.
- The University of Puerto Rico, Hamacoa, will improve training for new faculty and administrators to improve gender equity.
- The University of Colorado–Boulder will increase the number of women serving in administrative positions in science, mathematics, engineering, and technology programs through its Leadership Education for Advancement and Promotion Program.
- The University of Michigan is launching a campus climate initiative, a gender equity resource fund, and a department transformation initiative to provide interventions to improve opportunities for tenure-track women faculty in basic science and engineering fields.
- The University of Wisconsin–Madison is establishing a National Women in Science and Engineering Leadership Institute to gather data, monitor results, and disseminate information on the best practices for advancing women. As part of its chancellor's endowment goals, the university is including the creation of 10 professorships for the advancement of women in science and engineering.
- The University of California–Irvine will provide women a network of support and guidance through tenure and will set up a mentoring program for junior faculty. It will also establish two

ADVANCE chairs, to be awarded to tenured faculty in the sciences with strong academic credentials and a demonstrated commitment to gender equity.

Later in 2002, a ninth institution received the NSF Transformation Award: Hunter College–CUNY joins NSF in the goal of contributing to the development of a national science and engineering academic workforce that includes the full participation of women in all levels of faculty and academic administration, particularly at the senior academic ranks, through the transformation of institutional practices, policies, climate, and culture via is Gender Equity Project.

The second year of a 5-year award is too early to judge the success of these complex, institutional projects for attracting, retaining, and advancing women scientists and engineers. The focus in the press releases on improving the tenure process at Georgia Tech, New Mexico State, the University of Michigan, and UC–Irvine, combined with centers for institutional change, leadership, and gender equity at the University of Washington, the University of Puerto Rico, the University of Wisconsin–Madison, and the University of Colorado–Boulder, and professorships for senior women at almost all institutions suggests that ADVANCE holds significant potential. ADVANCE promises to go beyond individual research projects of women scientists and engineers that initiatives such as POWRE, FAW, CAA, and VPW supported to solve problems with broader systemic and institutional roots such as balancing career and family.

### Conclusions: Policy Recommendations and Considerations

Data from the almost 400 POWRE awardees, mostly at Research I and comprehensive institutions, coupled with those of the almost 50 CBL professors, mostly at small liberal arts colleges, who responded to an e-mail questionnaire provide insights into barriers that institutions must seek to remove, or at least lower, to increase the retention of women scientists and engineers and to attract more women to the disciplines. The experiences of the POWRE and CBL awardees, reflected in the e-mail questionnaires and interviews, suggest various policy considerations for removing the institutional barriers that prevent women from being full participants in science and technology disciplines. At least four distinct policy issues that emerge from the responses can inform ADVANCE and other institutional transformation projects. These can be organized around the 4 response categories, which evolved from grouping together similar responses across all four years of the study.

*Balancing Career and Family*

The most pressing, immediate concern that institutions must alleviate is the difficulty women face in balancing family and career. Though this issue affects many women (and increasingly men also), it is particularly challenging for women in competitive fields such as science and engineering (Wasserman, 2000). The conflicting demands of work and personal responsibilities are likely exacerbated for women science and engineering faculty because of the competitiveness and inflexibility characteristics of these fields. Engineering, in particular, with its foundation in the military, often perpetuates its hierarchical nature and cut-throat competitiveness, even though such characteristics are counterproductive to a supportive, balanced environment that would enable all faculty members to achieve their full potential.

The balancing act extends beyond the scenario of a woman juggling children and her job; it also impacts the woman's decision on when (or whether) to have children. For many women, the decision impacts their likelihood of getting tenure (Cook, 2001). Family friendly policies that stop the tenure clock, provide on-site daycare, and facilitate dual-career hires should help both men and women faculty (Wenniger, 2001; Wilson, 2001). American Association of University Professors [AAUP] policy is to stop the tenure clock for parental leave (available to men or women), postponing the time faculty come up for tenure. The University of California system-wide policy offers faculty an option called active service-modified duties, which permits a parent, spouse, or partner with substantial responsibilities for caring for a young child to request a quarter or semester of active service-modified duties around the time of birth or adoption (Cook, 2001). Since balancing the tenure clock with the biological clock challenges women scientists and engi-

neers who want to become biological mothers in ways never faced by
men, such policies will benefit women more.

In a similar fashion, since most (62%) female scientists and engineers are also married to male scientists or engineers, who are also
often in the same field, such women experience more problems with
the two-career issue (Williams, 2001) than their male colleagues, most
of whom are married, but not to women scientists and engineers (Sonnert & Holton, 1995). Although "balancing career with family" and
"dual career" relationships appear at first blush to be the result of the
individual choices made by women alone and/or in conjunction with
their spouse or partner, the predominance of these responses by
POWRE awardees from all 4 years and CBL professors in response to
an open-ended question suggests that addressing the problem at the
level of the individual proves inadequate. Institutional responses are
needed to resolve these family-centered issues identified by overwhelming numbers of women scientists.

Successful institutional solutions appear promising. Such solutions
cluster around two issues — increased flexibility for individual faculty
members and the distribution of control from the institution or administration to the individual. Flexibility evident in work hours, benefits,
and telecommuting and distribution of control to the individual
through a cafeteria system of benefits or in a start-up package that
includes a professional development account available until tenure
(hallmark of the CBL Professorships) exemplify such institutional
solutions.

Several institutions have developed a cafeteria of benefits that provides important flexibility across the span of a faculty member's career.
Child-care or elder-care benefits may take the form of financial assistance, information and assessment of available services, or the conve-
nience of on-site facilities. An example of this type of flexibility exists
at Iowa State University, where on-site child care for infants through
kindergartners has a sliding scale of fees; a cafeteria of benefits allows
any benefit dollars that remain after selection to be moved to a flexible
spending account for medical expenses or child-care expenses, departmental assistance for spousal hires, and lactation rooms for nursing
women.

A few institutions have begun to formalize policies to facilitate partner hires (Wilson, 2001). The University of Arizona, for example, has
taken a proactive stance by negotiating a set of guidelines for partner-
ship hires as a means to attract and retain couples; these guidelines
include provisions such as the provost or vice president paying up to
one-third of a partner's salary for 3 years, when funds are available
(Riley, 2001).

Institutional policies that address the issue of balance would likely
have a positive impact on the recruitment and retention of female
undergraduate and graduate students, as well. The perception that success in the sciences and engineering requires an unbalanced intense
focus on inanimate objects for prolonged periods of time is a significant
deterrent to women selecting those fields for a life-long career (Margolis & Fisher, 2002).

*Low Numbers of Women and Stereotyping*

Problems resulting from low numbers of women in science and engineering can lead to stereotypes surrounding their performance, isolation, lack of mentoring, and difficulty gaining credibility among their
peers and administrators. Such problems become increasingly complex
to address at the institutional level because of the considerable varia-
tions among fields. As the numbers of women have increased quite
markedly in some disciplines (psychology, sociology) and begun to
approach parity in others (life sciences), while remaining relatively
small in others (engineering and computer science), it may be important to focus on differences women face in different disciplines. Small
numbers make women very visible. Visibility draws attention to successful performance, but it also spotlights errors. The variance in numbers from field to field suggests that institutions may need to establish
different priorities and policies for women in different disciplines in
sciences and engineering. For example, a one-size-fits-all policy may
not work equally well for women in engineering compared to their
counterparts in biology. The ADVANCE institutions, along with several other institutions such as the University of Arizona (Riley, 2001),
are undertaking studies of salaries, space, and other resources provided
to women scientists and engineers on their campuses as a result of the

MIT report and the statement issued at the end of the January 29, 2001, meeting.

Continuing low numbers provide particular challenges and some opportunities. Because the unwritten rules of academia often go unlearned by women in academe until professional disaster strikes (Aisenberg & Harrington, 1988), increasing the number of women in science and engineering becomes even more critical to ensuring that such rules are learned. Low numbers mean that these women often serve as the first or one of few women in their department or college. They may have no senior women colleagues to act as role models and to serve as mentors to provide them access to networks of necessary professional information. These low numbers also lead to being asked to serve on more committees (even at the junior level) and to advise more students. Although these service activities provide opportunities for women to be visible and to experience leadership and administration at an early stage in their career, they may not be valued by the institution for promotion and tenure and may lead to difficulties with time management. Thus, it is crucial for the former Research I institutions to ensure either that junior women faculty are not given extra teaching and service, or that the tenure and promotion committees recognize and validate such work to compensate for lost research time and focus. The NSF has articulated that the relatively large size of ADVANCE awards emerged from the recognition of a need to signal the importance of this work by women to build the infrastructure of the scientific and engineering communities (Alice Hogan, personal communication, October 18, 2002)

Understanding specific characteristics of gender differences at each institution and within individual departments provides a first step to widening paths. Do paths narrow in certain places (departments), at certain distances (recruitment, tenure, promotion to full professor, prestigious awards, influential committees), or at specific points (salary, space, graduate student assignment)? Surveys such as the ones conducted at MIT (Hopkins, Bailyn, Gibson, & Hammonds, 2002) identified sources of inequity that further restricted the already narrow paths to successful advancement and recognition for women faculty.

Creating additional, equally valued paths to success also widens career opportunities. A brainstorming meeting or survey of beginning faculty and graduate students provides alternatives to the traditional procedures for advancement and recognition that may be more effective for future faculty members. Alternative paths to success must be seen by the academic community as equally prestigious and attractive to faculty regardless of gender, age, race, or ethnicity.

Providing more structure and transparency to the advancement and recognition practices in individual departments also widens paths. Negative forms of discrimination are less likely to occur if the paths to academic advancement and recognition are clearly understood by both the beginning faculty members who must negotiate them and the senior faculty responsible for their implementation (Fox, 1995). Examples of such transparency include a panel of newly tenured faculty speaking to new faculty or an effective 3rd-year review process that identifies potential weaknesses in an untenured faculty member and provides a plan for addressing those weaknesses.

### Overt Discrimination and Harassment

The low numbers that result in active recruitment of women into many areas may have both positive and negative consequences. Demand may give women engineers starting salaries that are equal to or higher than those of their male counterparts (Vetter, 1996). The negative perception of affirmative action policies and active recruitment of women can lead to various forms of backlash, ranging from overt discrimination to difficulties gaining credibility from peers and administrators who assume a woman obtained the position to fill a quota.

The situations of overt and subtle harassment that women encounter must be dealt with at the institutional level. Institutions and professional societies need to establish policies against sexual harassment and gender discrimination, including against pregnant faculty in hiring, promotion, and tenure if such policies do not exist (Elliot, 2001). Flexibility and acceptance of differences between men and women may be crucial not only for retaining and advancing the numbers of women and careers of individual women in sciences and engineering, but such tolerance may also serve as the key for new approaches to collaboration and creative generativity.

Institutional policies against sexual harassment and gender discrimination must be implemented and enforced. Senior administrators play critical roles in terms of allocation of human, financial, physical, and time rewards for those who enforce such policies. For example, giving the outstanding research award from the university and/or providing a research sabbatical are not appropriate for a documented harasser as mechanisms to get him or her out of a problem situation. Upon rare occasions, where the senior administrator is the harasser, the institution must be particularly responsible to ensure that action is taken. Indiana University–South Bend demoted Daniel Cohen from his position as chancellor after he lost a sexual harassment suit. When the faculty voted not to censure him, current Chancellor Kenneth Perrin banned Cohen from campus (Wenninger, 2001). In many fields, sexual harassment and gender discrimination workshops should include substantial focus on cultural/national differences regarding gender roles and expectations in U.S. universities for appropriate professional behavior, including collaboration with women colleagues.

*Decreased Funding Issues*

Trends toward tightening the federal budget for research and the resulting competitive environment impacts both men and women scientists and engineers. However, women may face a disproportionate disadvantage in this area due to issues related to their low numbers and family-balancing act. Women also tend to work in teams more than men. Though a recent trend is toward more collaborative research, the need to establish oneself as an independent researcher is critical to securing grants and funding; thus, women may actually be less successful if they tend to collaborate. Women are also socialized to be less overtly competitive — a trait often associated with success — which may increase their difficulty for success in a highly competitive environment. Thus, the lack of social and professional connections available to most women in academic science and engineering departments, overt and covert gender bias, and differences in socialization create special and unique problems for women (Fox, 2001).

To enhance funding opportunities, academic departments can develop grant-writing seminars for new and even existing faculty or encourage faculty to attend existing seminars offered through campus offices of sponsored research. Although collaboration should be encouraged for all faculty where research topics deem it appropriate, institutions must also foster women's independent research. Retention of the Fellows Awards category within ADVANCE continues the opportunity provided by POWRE for women to receive support for their independent research initiatives after their careers have been interrupted (NSF, 2001b).

Words describing the environment encountered by women faculty in science and engineering departments include chilly, masculine, exclusionary, elitist, and hostile. Is it any wonder that, even in fields such as chemistry, where the proportion of women completing Ph.D.s has been above 20% since 1985 (American Chemical Society, 1999) the proportion of those choosing to return to the inhospitable environments that educated them is closer to 12% at the top 50 universities (Chemical and Engineering News, 2002)? Instead of nurturing the women who successfully complete the competitive, often grueling educational and postdoctoral experiences, senior faculty may erect additional obstacles and artificial measures of quality to exclude the very people who might add new ways of thinking to improve the educational environment.

Wadsworth (2002) suggests other ways of improving the environment in *Giving Much, Gaining More*. The book describes the personal impact of mentoring programs developed at Purdue University in the 1990s that successfully used positive actions to offset the negative characteristics of engineering departments — welcoming vs. excluding, communicating vs. bickering, trusting vs. doubting, accepting vs. rejecting, and affirming vs. ridiculing. If such positive actions became the "norm" in science and engineering departments, the need for such supplemental support programs for women would eventually disappear.

Recognition of these policy issues is only a first step in overcoming the institutional barriers that keep women from fully participating in science and technology. The POWRE and CBL data and interviews provide important information for policymakers at the institutional level as well as for national professional societies and foundations to identify and implement appropriate interventions; they suggest that unleashing the talent within women scientists and engineers is advanced by institutional policies and guidelines such as those offered above. The tremendous love for science and technology and extreme dedication to their research and profession strongly characterize the responses of the overwhelming majority of POWRE and CBL awardees. Most seek to have the barriers removed so they can be productive researchers who take creative approaches to the physical, natural world.

NSF's recent ADVANCE awards for institutional transformation include attempts to change the environment for women in the sciences and engineering. The results of ADVANCE will provide a variety of models for improving the environment in academic science and engineering departments and transform faculty careers to be more attractive and supportive of all men and women, particularly those from previously underrepresented populations.

# References

Aisenberg, N., & Harrington, M. (1988). *Women of academe: Outsiders in the sacred grove.* Washington, DC: Joseph Henry Press.

Allaire, Y., & Firsirotu, M. (1984). Theories of organizational culture. *Organization Studies, 5,* 193–226.

Ambrose, S., Dunkle, K., Lazarus, B., Nair, I., & Harkus, D. (1997). *Journeys of women in science and engineering: No universal constants.* Philadelphia: Temple University Press.

American Association for the Advancement of Science (AAAS). (1990). *Science for all Americans.* Washington, DC:

American Association for the Advancement of Science (AAAS). (1993). *Benchmarks for science literacy.* New York: Oxford University Press.

American Association of University Women. (1992). *How schools shortchange girls.* Washington, DC: AAUW Educational Foundation.

American Chemical Society. (1999). Percentage of chemistry degrees earned by women from 1967 to 1999. *ACS Starting Salary Survey.* retrieved October 1, 2001 from http://center.acs.org/applications/acscomparator.

Barad, K. (1995). A feminist approach to teaching quantum physics. In S. V. Rosser (Ed.), *Teaching the majority* Pp. 43–75. Teachers College Press. New York.

Bohonak, N. (1995). Attracting and retaining women in graduate programs in computer science. In S. V. Rosser (Ed.), *Teaching the majority.* New York: Teachers College Press.

Britton, D. M. (1997). Perceptions of the work environment among correctional officers: Do race and sex matter? *Criminology, 35,* 75–105.

Bush, V. (1945). *Science—The endless frontier: A report to the president on a program for postwar scientific research.* Reprinted 1990. Washington, DC: National Science Foundation.

Campbell, K. (2001). Leaders of 9 universities and 25 women faculty meet at MIT, agree to equity reviews. *MIT News Office.* Retrieved January 31, 2001 from http://web.mit.edu/newsoffice/nr/2001/gender.html.

Carroll, B. (2001). Reflections on "2000 subversions: Women's studies and the 21st century." *NWSA Journal 13*(1), 139–149.

*Chemical and Engineering News.* (2002, September). 110–111.

Clutter, M. (1998). Background programs to POWRE. Appendix B. In S. V. Rosser & M. L. Zieseniss (Eds.), *Final report on professional opportunities for women in research and education (POWRE) workshop.* Gainesville, FL: Center for Women's Studies and Gender Research.

Commission on Professionals in Science & Technology. (2000). *Professional women & minorities: A total resources data compendium.* 13th ed. Washington, DC: Author.

Cook, S. G. (2001). Negotiating family accommodation practices on your campus. *Women in Higher Education, 10*(4); 25–26.

Curry, D. (2001, July 6). Prime numbers. *The Chronicle of Higher Education*, A9.

Davis, C. S., Ginorio, A. B., Hollenshead, C. S., Lazarus, B. B., Rayman, P. M., & Associates (Eds.). (1996). *The equity equation: Fostering the advancement of women in the sciences, mathematics and engineering.* San Francisco: Jossey-Bass.

DeGroot, J., & Maynard, M. (1993). *Women's studies in the 1990's: Doing things differently?* New York: St. Martin's Press.

Eastman, C. (1995). Accommodating diversity in computer science education. In S. V. Rosser, (Ed.), *Teaching the majority* (pp. 160–168). Teachers College Press. New York.

Edsall, T. (1995, August 15). Pollsters view gender gap as political fixture: White men heed GOP call; women lean to democrats. *Washington Post*, A–1.

Elliott, S. T. (2001). Does your school discriminate against pregnant faculty? *Women in Higher Education, 10*(7); 23–24.

Fox, M. (1985). Publication, performance, and reward in science and scholarship. In J. Smart (Ed.), *Higher education: Handbook of theory and research* (pp. 255–282). New York: Agathon Press.

Fox, M. (1991). Gender, environment milieu, and productivity in science and scholarship. In H. Zuckerman, J. Cole, & J. Bruer (Eds.), *The outer circle: Women in the scientific community* (pp. 188–204). New York: W. W. Norton.

Fox, M. (1995). Women and scientific careers. In S. Jasanoff, J. Marble, J. Petersen, & T. Pinch (Eds.). *Handbook of science and technology studies* (pp. 205–233). Newbury Park, CA: Sage.

Fox, M. (1996). Women, academia and careers in science. In C. S. Davis, A. B. Ginorio, C. S. Hollenshead, B. B. Lazarus, P. M. Rayman, & Associates (Eds.), *The equity equation: Fostering the advancement of women in the sciences, mathematics, and engineering* (pp. 265–269). San Francisco: Jossey–Bass.

Fox, M. (2001). Women, men, and engineering. In D. Vannoy (Ed.), *Gender Mosaics* (pp. 249–257). Los Angeles: Roxbury.

Glazer, P., & Slater, M. (1987). *Unequal colleagues.* New Brunswick, NJ: Rutgers University Press.

Heckman, D. (1997, Winter). On the eve of Title IX's 25th anniversary: Sex discrimination in the gym and classroom. *Nova Law Review, 21*, 545–661.

Henry Luce Foundation. (2000). *The Clare Boothe Luce program for women in science, mathematics and engineering.* New York. Author.

Hopkins, N. (1999, December 3). MIT and gender bias: Following up on victory. *Chronicle of Higher Education.* Vol. XLVI, No. 15, B–4.

Hopkins, N. Bailyn, L., Gibson, L., & Hammonds, E. (2002). *The status of women faculty at MIT.* Retrieved from http://web.mit.edu/faculty/reports/overview.html.

Keller, E. F. (1983). *A feeling for the organism: The life and work of Barbara McClintock.* New York: W.H. Freeman.

Keller, E. F. (1985). *Reflections on gender and science.* New Haven, CT: Yale University Press.

Kole, A. (1995, August 3). *Highlights of the Affirmative Action Review—Report to the president by the office of the general counsel.* Washington, DC: Department of Education.

Kulis, S., Sciotte, D., & Collins, S. (2002). More than a pipeline problem. Labor constraints and gender stratification across the scientific disciplines. *Journal of Research in Higher Education, 43*(6), 657–691.

Latour, B., & Woolgar, S. (1979). *Laboratory life: The social construction of scientific facts.* Beverly Hills, CA: Sage Publications.

Latour, B. (1987). *Science in action.* Cambridge, MA: Harvard University Press.

Lauer, N. C. (2000, July 18). Judge upholds Bush's anti-affirmative action plan. *Women's Enews.* Retrieved May 1, 2001, from http://www.womensenews.org.

Margolis, J., & Fisher, A. (2002). *Unlocking the clubhouse*. Cambridge, MA: MIT Press.

McIlwee, J., & Robinson, J. G. (1992). *Women in engineering: Gender, power and workplace culture*. Albany, NY: SUNY Press.

McIntosh, P. (1984). The study of women: Processes of personal and curricular revision. *Forum for Liberal Education, 6*(5); 2–4.

McNeil, L., & Sher, M. (1999). The dual-career couple problem. *Physics Today, 52*(7), 32–37.

National Research Council. (1996). *National Science Education Standards*. Washington, DC: National Academy Press.

National Science Board. (2000). *Science & Engineering Indicators—2000* (NSB-00-1). Arlington, VA: National Science Foundation.

National Science Foundation. (1993). *Education and human resources program for women and girls program announcement* (NSF 93-126) Arlington, VA: Author.

National Science Foundation. (1994). *Women, minorities, and persons with disabilities in science and engineering: 1994*. (NSF 94-333). Washington, DC: National Science Foundation.

National Science Foundation. (1997). *Professional opportunities for women in research and education*. Program announcement (NSF 97-91). Arlington, VA: Author.

National Science Foundation. (2000). *Women, minorities, and persons with disabilities in science and engineering*: 2000 (NSF 00–327). Arlington, VA: Author.

National Science Foundation. (2001a). *Program for gender equity in science, mathematics, engineering and technology (PGE)*. Program Announcement (NSF 01-6). Arlington, VA: Author.

National Science Foundation. (2001b). *ADVANCE. Program solicitation*. Arlington, VA: Author.

National Science Foundation. (2001c). *ADVANCE institutional transformation awards*. Retrieved October 1, 2001 from http://www.nsf.gov/advance.

National Science Foundation. (2003). *Gender diversity in science, technology engineering and mathematics education (GDSE)* Program Announcement (NSF 03–502). Arlington, VA: Author.

National Science Foundation. (in press). *Women, minorities, and persons with disabilities in science and engineering*.

Project Kaleidoscope. 1994. *Project kaleidoscope phase II: What works: Focusing on the future*. Washington, DC: Independent Colleges Office.

Pryse, M., Chair, and Members of the Task Force on Faculty Roles and Rewards of the National Women's Studies Association. (1999). *Defining women's studies scholarship*. A statement of the National Women's Studies Association Task Force on Faculty Roles and Rewards. College Park, MD: National Women's Studies Association.

Richard, G. V., & Krieshok, T. S. (1989). Occupational stress, strain, and coping in university faculty. *Journal of Vocational Behavior, 34*, 117–132.

Richardson, D., Sutton, C., & Cercone, K. (1995). Female–friendly geoscience: Eight techniques for reaching the majority. In S. V. Rosser (Ed.), *Teaching the majority*. pp. 183–192. New York: Teachers College Press.

Riley, M. D. (2001). U. of Arizona's millenium project to assess campus equity. *Women in higher education, 10*(4); 1–2.

Rosser, S. V. (1990). *Female friendly science*. Elmsford, NY: Pergamon Press.

Rosser, S. V. (1995). *Teaching the majority: Breaking the gender barrier in science, mathematics, and engineering*. New York: Teachers College Press.

Rosser, S. V. (1997). *Re-engineering female friendly science*. Elmsford, NY: Pergamon Press.

Rosser, S. V. (1999). Different laboratory/work climates: Impacts upon women in the workplace. In C. Selby (Ed.), *Women in science and engineering: Choices for success. Annals of the New York Academy of Sciences* (pp. 95–101).

Rosser, S. V. (2001). Balancing: Survey of fiscal year 1997, 1998, and 1999 POWRE award-ees. *Journal of Women and Minorities in Science and Engineering, 7*(1); 1–11.

Rosser, S. V. & Lane, E. O'Neal. (2002). Key barriers for academic institutions seeking to retain women scientists and engineers: Family unfriendly policies, low numbers, ste-reotypes, and harassment. *Journal of Women and Minorities in Science and Engineering, 8*(2); pp. 163–191.

Rosser, S. V., & Zieseniss, M. (1998). *Final report on professional opportunities for women in research and education (POWRE) workshop.* Gainesville, FL: Center for Women's Stud-ies and Gender Research.

Rosser, S. V., & Zieseniss, M. (2000). Career issues and laboratory climates: Different chal-lenges and opportunities for women engineers and scientists (Survey of fiscal year 1997 POWRE Awardees). *Journal of Women and Minorities in Science and Engineering, 6*(2); 1–20.

Sandler, B. (1997, Spring). Too strong for a woman: The five words that created Title IX. *About Women on Campus, 5*(2); 5.

Schneider, A. (2000, August 18). Female scientists turn their backs on jobs at research uni-versities. *Chronicle of Higher Education,* A12–A14.

Schuster, M., & Van Dyne, S. (1984). Placing women in the liberal arts: Stages of curricu-lum transformation. *Harvard Educational Review,* 54(4); 413–428.

Solomon, B. M. (1985). *In the company of educated women.* New Haven, CT: Yale University Press.

Sonnert, G., & Holton, G. (1995). *Who succeeds in science? The gender dimension.* New Brun-swick, NJ: Rutgers University Press.

SRI International. (1994). *The visiting professorships for women program: lowering the hurdles for women in science and engineering.* NSF Summary and Comments (NSF 93-159). Arlington, VA: Author.

Swoboda, F. (1995, March 16). Glass ceiling firmly in place, panel finds. Washington Post, A1, A18.

Tobias, S. (1990). *They're not dumb, they're different.* Tucson, AZ: Research Corporation.

Tobias, S. (1992). *Revitalizing undergraduate science education: Why some things work and most don't.* Tucson, AZ: Research Corporation.

Traweek, S. (1988). *Beamtimes and lifetimes: The world of high energy physics.* Cambridge, MA: Harvard University Press.

Valian, V. (1998). *Why so slow? The advancement of women.* Cambridge, MA: MIT Press.

Vetter, B. (1996). Myths and realities of women's progress in the sciences, mathematics, and engineering. In C. S. Davis, A. B. Ginorio, C. S. Hollenshead, B. B. Lazarus, P. M. Rayman, & Associates (Eds.) *The equity equation: Fostering the advancement of women in the sciences, mathematics, and engineering* (pp. 29–56). San Francisco: Jossey-Bass.

Wadsworth, E. (2002). *Giving much, gaining more.* West Lafayette, IN: Purdue University Press.

Wasserman, E. R. (1998). Women in the national academy: Their lives as scientists and as women. *Magazine of the Association of Women in Science, 27,* 6–10.

Wasserman, E. R. (2000). *The door in the dream: Conversations with eminent women in Sci-ence.* Washington, DC: Joseph Henry Press.

Wenniger, M.D. (2001). Partner hires: A fact of life on most campuses. *Women in Higher Education 10*(4): 5.

Williams, J. (2001, December 15). What stymies women's academic careers? It's hiring cou-ples. *The Chronicle of Higher Education,* B10.

Wilson, R. (2001, April 13). The backlash against hiring couples. *Chronicle of Higher Educa-tion,* A16.

Wright, K. N., & Saylor, W. G. (1992). A comparison of perceptions of the work environment between minority and non-minority employees of the federal prison system. *Journal of Criminal Justice, 20*(1), 63 – 71.

Zimmerman, B. (2000). Building NWSA. *NWSA Journal, 12*(1); 165–168.

# Index